D0142738

DRAKE MEMORIAL LIBRARY
WITHDRAWN
THE COLLEGE AT BROCKPORT

Judith A. Margolin

Breaking the Silence
Group Therapy
for Childhood Sexual Abuse

A Practitioner's Manual

Pre-publication
REVIEWS,
COMMENTARIES,
EVALUATIONS . . .

"**D**r. Margolin's well-written book offers professionals information and skills that are essential to conducting successful groups for adult survivors of childhood sexual abuse. She provides an up-to-date review of the current knowledge base in the field. In addition, she offers a nuts-and-bolts description of the therapy approach from the assessment process to group termination and includes useful questionnaires and hand-outs. The book effectively prepares therapists for the potential struggles faced by both group participants and therapists by means of powerful and complex case examples. While structured and educational in format, the group therapy program described offers the skills, support, and flexibility that enable survivors to heal themselves, while also fostering the healing of other group members. This book is an extremely valuable resource for all therapists working with adult survivors of childhood sexual abuse."

Esther Deblinger, PhD
Associate Professor
of Clinical Psychiatry,
University of Medicine
and Dentistry of New Jersey
School of Osteopathic Medicine

"**I**n her preface the author promises 'a basic guide for those first beginning to run groups, so that they do not have to reinvent the wheel.' I am happy to report she keeps her promise. Margolin has provided the reader with easily understood practical information. She cites the professional literature enough to show how her methods fit well within current thinking, but does not get bogged down in details or controversies. There is enough information here to stimulate, but not overwhelm the reader.

The target population is adults who 'report involvement in incestuous and sexually abusive relationships during childhood, who are currently involved in individual psychotherapy, and who are not actively psychotic, suicidal, or substance abusing.'

She realizes that the effects of sexual abuse will not be eliminated in fifteen psychoeducational sessions. Her overall goal is to 'provide a structured, safe environment to be used as a springboard for future therapeutic work' in which the clients are able to 'break the secrecy and decrease the feelings of guilt, blame, and shame surrounding the incestuous experience.' Protocols for each of the sessions are included. Margolin provides the rationale for including each topic, the goals and objectives, the materials needed, and the procedures to be used. In addition, the goals of each session are illustrated through the use of case examples. Topics covered are: trust and safety, exploration of emotions and beliefs, disclosure of abuse, the aftermath of abuse, family dynamics, sexuality and intimacy, processing memories, and group termination. Her thirty-six item questionnaire would prove helpful in assisting clients in identifying the impact of childhood sexual abuse on their current life.

The issues of male survivors are addressed throughout the book, rather than merely being included in a brief separate section as do so many books on sexual abuse.

I can wholeheartedly recommend this book to beginning therapists, and even to those with experience facilitating psychoeducational groups on childhood sexual abuse."

Mic Hunter, PsyD
*Licensed Psychologist
and Marriage and Family Therapist,
Internationally Certified Drug
and Alcohol Counselor*

More pre-publication
REVIEWS, COMMENTARIES, EVALUATIONS . . .

"**G**roup therapy has long been recognized as a powerful and potent treatment modality. Now with *Breaking the Silence,* there is a practical, theory-based group manual for conducting short-term psychoeducational groups for adults who have experienced childhood sexual abuse. In keeping with current literature and evolving standards of care, Judith Margolin has developed a paced and well-formulated cognitive-behavioral protocol. While survivors are encouraged to share their stories, the group focuses primarily on developing coping skills, enhancing self-care abilities, and exploring the impact, meaning, and aftereffects of sexual abuse.

Margolin provides a straightforward and detailed manual that includes the rationale, goals and objectives, materials needed, and structure for each group session, including verbatim leader instructions. In addition, the author considers other critical variables such as the group's potential to overwhelm, selection criteria for membership, organizational support, and the complex issue of memory and memory recall. This nuts-and-bolts, step-by-step manual takes the anxiety out of the mix for the beginning therapist. It will also be a valuable resource for the seasoned veteran who has never facilitated a group for adults of childhood sexual abuse. This book is sure to make offering psychoeducational groups a more viable treatment option."

Marsha L. Heiman, PhD
Clinical Coordinator,
Child Sexual Abuse Case
Consultation Project,
New Jersey Task Force
on Child Abuse and Neglect

HMTP

The Haworth Maltreatment and Trauma Press
An Imprint of The Haworth Press, Inc.
New York • London

NOTES FOR PROFESSIONAL LIBRARIANS
AND LIBRARY USERS

This is an original book title published by The Haworth Maltreatment and Trauma Press, an imprint of The Haworth Press, Inc. Unless otherwise noted in specific chapters with attribution, materials in this book have not been previously published elsewhere in any format or language.

CONSERVATION AND PRESERVATION NOTES

All books published by The Haworth Press, Inc. and its imprints are printed on certified pH neutral, acid free book grade paper. This paper meets the minimum requirements of American National Standard for Information Sciences–Permanence of Paper for Printed Material, ANSI Z39.48-1984.

Breaking the Silence

Group Therapy
for Childhood Sexual Abuse

A Practitioner's Manual

THE HAWORTH MALTREATMENT AND TRAUMA PRESS
Robert A. Geffner, PhD
Senior Editor

New, Recent, and Forthcoming Titles:

Sexual, Physical, and Emotional Abuse in Out-of-Home Care: Prevention Skills for At-Risk Children by Toni Cavanagh Johnson and Associates

Cedar House: A Model Child Abuse Treatment Program by Bobbi Kendig with Clara Lowry

Bridging Worlds: Understanding and Facilitating Adolescent Recovery from the Trauma of Abuse by Joycee Kennedy and Carol McCarthy

The Learning About Myself (LAMS) Program for At-Risk Parents: Learning from the Past—Changing the Future by Verna Rickard

The Learning About Myself (LAMS) Program for At-Risk Parents: Handbook for Group Participants by Verna Rickard

Treating Children with Sexually Abusive Behavior Problems: Guidelines for Child and Parent Intervention by Jan Ellen Burton, Lucinda A. Rasmussen, Julie Bradshaw, Barbara J. Christopherson, and Steven C. Huke

Bearing Witness: Violence and Collective Responsibility by Sandra L. Bloom and Michael Reichert

Sibling Abuse Trauma: Assessment and Intervention Strategies for Children, Families, and Adults by John V. Caffaro and Allison Conn-Caffaro

From Surviving to Thriving: A Therapist's Guide to Stage II Recovery for Survivors of Childhood Abuse by Mary Bratton

"I Never Told Anyone This Before": Managing the Initial Disclosure of Sexual Abuse Re-Collections by Janice A. Gasker

Breaking the Silence: Group Therapy for Childhood Sexual Abuse, A Practitioner's Manual by Judith A. Margolin

Stopping the Violence: A Group Model to Change Men's Abusive Attitude and Behaviors by David J. Decker

Stopping the Violence: A Group Model to Change Men's Abusive Attitude and Behaviors—The Client Workbook by David J. Decker

Breaking the Silence
Group Therapy
for Childhood Sexual Abuse

A Practitioner's Manual

Judith A. Margolin

HMTP

The Haworth Maltreatment and Trauma Press
An Imprint of The Haworth Press, Inc.
New York • London

Published by

The Haworth Maltreatment and Trauma Press, an imprint of The Haworth Press, Inc., 10 Alice Street, Binghamton, NY 13904-1580

© 1999 by The Haworth Press, Inc. All rights reserved. No part of this work may be reproduced or utilized in any form or by any means, electronic or mechanical, including photocopying, microfilm, and recording, or by any information storage and retrieval system, without permission in writing from the publisher. Printed in the United States of America.

Cover design by Monica L. Seifert.

Library of Congress Cataloging-in-Publication Data

Margolin, Judith A.
   Breaking the silence : group therapy for childhood sexual abuse : a practitioner's manual/ Judith A. Margolin.
      p.   cm.
   Includes bibliographical references and index.
   ISBN 0-7890-0200-0 (alk. paper)
   1. Adult child sexual abuse victims—Handbooks, manuals, etc.   2. Group psychothera- py—Handbooks, manuals, etc. I. Title.
RC569.5.A28M37 1999
616.85′83690651—dc21   98-39343
                                                                                             CIP

To my family, Moshe, Ayelet, Gidon, and Noa
... for their love, support, and patience

ABOUT THE AUTHOR

Judith A. Margolin, PsyD, is a licensed psychologist in private practice in Freehold and Kingston, New Jersey. Dr. Margolin is also visiting faculty at the Graduate School of Applied and Professional Psychology of Rutgers University, as well as a member of the Speaker's Bureau of the Governor's Task Force on Child Abuse. In addition, Dr. Margolin has consulted in area school districts as an advocate for children and families. Her professional interests include, in particular, trauma and abuse, the adolescent female, and women's issues. She is the author or co-author of several journal articles and has presented on a variety of topics at professional conferences.

CONTENTS

PART II: SESSION PROTOCOLS

Chapter 5. The Screening Intake   **55**

Chapter 6. The Group Sessions   **61**

Chapter 7. Special Topics   **109**

Preface

Breaking the Silence has been in development for over five years. It began as a germ of an idea during the early summer of 1991 and grew to its present form through numerous revisions. The program was developed in response to an appeal from a member of the college community at a Northeastern university. At the time, few groups were available for women who had been sexually molested as children. The few campus groups addressing this need were limited to undergraduate students only and were run in a very unstructured, open-ended manner. Graduate students, and other women in the community at large, were unable to find any resources that could address their particular needs, time demands, and added responsibilities. Based upon this request, my colleagues and I decided to meet their needs within our training clinic at Rutgers University.

Excited by the prospect, yet lacking an adequate knowledge base, my colleagues and I set about combing the available literature on group therapy for survivors of sexual abuse. In addition to the theoretical background information, we had hoped to discover some basic "how-tos" to facilitate our beginning venture. Instead, we found a dearth of practical, step-by-step material. We soon realized that we had to start at square one and reinvent the wheel already invented by other professionals working with this population. What we did discover was that group therapy was overwhelmingly recommended as the treatment of choice for this population, either independently or as adjunctive treatment. Key components and issues relating to conducting groups for survivors were repeatedly addressed in the literature, however unsystematically. These elements included generic as well as abuse-specific concerns, such as membership, size, length of program, gender of therapists, safety, and treatment goals.

It was our task to integrate this knowledge into a format that would provide effective treatment for our clients. What emerged over the next three years is reflected in this practical program manual. Development of the program began with a detailed needs assessment that surveyed professionals who provided psychological services, and survivors themselves. A curriculum guide, beginning with the earliest steps involved in establishing the group, covering each detailed session, and terminating with an evaluation plan, was developed based on the needs identified in this survey. As additional needs of our community of adult women sexually abused as children were specified, components of the program were further revised, refined, and fine-tuned.

This concise, fifteen-session, time-limited, psychoeducational group therapy program for adult survivors of sexual abuse emerged as the final product. It is designed to therapeutically address the long-term sequelae associated with a past history of childhood sexual abuse. The program is composed of both psychoeducational and process-oriented components and is directed toward integrating the effect of the past abuse with the individual's current functioning. Issues identified in the literature, by professionals working with this population, and by the survivors themselves, are a primary focus for discussions and other interventions within the group setting.

This program provides a theoretically based, structured, and explicit model for conducting a group psychotherapy program for adult survivors of childhood sexual abuse. It is intended as a basic guide for those who are beginning their first groups in this field, so that they do not have to "reinvent the wheel." The program is intended to be a model that can be adapted to meet the needs of each unique group and the style of the therapist conducting the program.

Chapter 1 provides a review of the literature in the areas of trauma and the effects of sexual abuse. A cognitive framework is provided as a basis for this group work. Chapter 2 reviews the literature on current approaches of treatment for childhood sexual abuse. Group treatment is presented as the treatment of choice.

Chapter 3 discusses the prerequisites to successful program development. Identifying the needs of the group members allows flexible adaptation of the program to address their concerns. This can be accomplished through the use of a preliminary needs and context assessment. Also reviewed are some of the problems encountered in conducting a group of this nature. Chapter 4 directly addresses the "nitty-gritty" of getting started, highlighting the programmatic issues undergirding implementation.

The second section of the book, Chapters 5 and 6, consists of detailed protocols for each session of the fifteen-week group. These guides outline procedures from the initial intake session through the final termination. Additional topical issues are then addressed in Chapter 7 to provide supplementary information for the beginning group therapist.

Finally, the four appendixes found in the final section of the book serve to facilitate the adaptation and evaluation of the group program. The supplements in Appendix A enable readers to conduct their own needs assessment surveys as a way of adapting the program to meet their specific requirements. Appendixes B, C, and D include questionnaires for evaluating the success of each individual session, the program as a whole, and its enduring benefit.

Judith A. Margolin

Acknowledgments

This book has been through a prolonged gestation and birthing process, and its emergence has been guided by a number of talented, supportive, and encouraging midwives. I am indebted, first and foremost, to all the women who have participated in the groups upon which this program is based. This includes the survivors themselves, as well as my cotherapists, Drs. Betsey Westover and Jennifer Oppenheim. Their contributions have been invaluable; without their initial input, this book would never have been written.

Drs. Kenneth Schneider and Nancy Harrison of the Graduate School of Applied and Professional Psychology at Rutgers University have been much appreciated and valued mentors. Their assistance, encouragement, pertinent suggestions, and constructive criticism have guided this program's development. Dr. Robert Geffner's editorial feedback has allowed the manuscript to assume its present form.

I am most grateful to my family and friends, who have labored alongside me as this book was first conceived and then delivered. My husband, Moshe Margolin, has been my most ardent supporter, editor, and critic all along the way; my children have maintained their sense of humor through it all. Their belief in me has sustained me throughout this, at times, arduous endeavor.

Finally, I must acknowledge my father's contribution to the creation of this book. Although he has not lived to see its publication, it was his influence and guidance during my formative years that has enabled me to dream—and to believe that dreams do come true.

PART I:
BACKGROUND

Chapter 1

The Trauma
of Childhood Sexual Abuse

The experience of childhood sexual abuse (CSA) may be one of the most traumatic events endured by young people in our society, shattering assumptions about safety, trust, and invulnerability to harm. Developmental tasks may be compromised since multiple domains are affected. The child struggles to form attachments and basic trust as primary relationships are disrupted. The development of self-identity, bodily regulation, initiative, and intimacy are often threatened as ordinary adaptation to everyday life becomes overwhelming in the face of the traumatic experience. The response to this trauma should not necessarily be viewed as pathological but rather as a natural response to an unnatural situation (McCann and Pearlman, 1990; Herman, 1992; van der Kolk, 1987a).

As professionals, we need to identify the factors that influence or determine how children may respond to this experience. What permits one child to emerge seemingly unscathed, while another may be severely incapacitated? How does the meaning of the event to the individual influence the ability to survive this injury? How are these wounds carried forth into adulthood, and what is necessary to help one move beyond the hurt, pain, and dysfunction the trauma has wrought? Over the past few decades, numerous researchers have begun to answer these questions about the impact of childhood sexual abuse.

DEFINITION OF SEXUAL ABUSE

One of the first steps in studying this problem is reaching a uniformly accepted definition of the subject matter. Past investigators have defined childhood sexual abuse consistently as any exploitive sexual activity, ranging from fondling to intercourse, be-

tween a child and a person at least five years older, in which the
sexual contact is inflicted upon the child for the perpetrator's grati-
fication (Briere, 1992; Gelinas, 1983; Sgroi, 1988). Following these
same guidelines for the purpose of this manual, sexual abuse is
herein defined as any sexual behaviors with minor children, whether wanted or unwanted, that occurred when there was a power
differential or significant age difference between the persons involved (Sgroi, 1988). Any possible relationship is betrayed by the
older, more powerful person's use of the child for personal satisfaction.

PREVALENCE

Numerous researchers (Courtois, 1988; Alpert, 1990; Finkelhor,
1990; Herman, 1992; Briere, 1992) have documented the prevalence of childhood sexual abuse. Despite the consensus that the
occurrence of childhood sexual abuse is extensive, actual estimates
of adults who were sexually abused as children vary widely, ranging from 6 percent to 62 percent (Finkelhor, 1990). This wide range
may be due, in part, to differences in the definitions of sexual abuse,
population characteristics, and methodological variations involved
in obtaining reports of the abuse (Alpert, 1990). Russell's (1986)
random survey of 930 women indicated that 38 percent have experienced contact sexual abuse by an adult relative or stranger prior to
eighteen years of age. One to four percent of women have experienced father-daughter incest (Goodwin, 1982; Russell, 1986). Recent estimates place the sexual victimization rate around 20 to 30
percent for females and 10 to 15 percent for males (Finkelhor et al.,
1989; Coker, 1990; Briere, 1992).

The prevalence of sexual abuse victims in psychiatric populations is higher, with as many as 53 percent of adult female psychiatric inpatients and 30 to 50 percent of outpatients reporting incest
experiences in childhood (Goodwin, 1990; Carmen, Reiker, and
Mills, 1984; Alpert, 1990). A possible explanation for this is that
the psychiatric disorders most closely associated with a childhood
history of sexual abuse may reflect impairments in self- and social
functioning. The sexually abusive experience may have interfered
with developmental transitions necessary for an intact sense of self

and healthy interpersonal functioning (Cole and Putnam, 1992). The severity of psychiatric difficulties may be a function of the timing of the interference, as well as other contextual factors, such as the child's coping ability and the familial context.

EARLY AND LONG-TERM EFFECTS OF SEXUAL ABUSE

There is a lack of prospective data about the emotional sequelae of sexual abuse (Sgroi and Bunk, 1988). Current knowledge about effects of sexual abuse is based primarily on retrospective studies of troubled populations, in which a majority were sexually abused as children.

Browne and Finkelhor (1986) summarized the research on sexual abuse and confirmed the presence of a variety of initial effects and symptoms in this population, including fear, anxiety, depression, anger, aggression, and sexually inappropriate behavior. Long-term effects frequently noted in initial research have affected the individual's functioning in a number of domains:

- Emotional responses
- Self-perception and identity
- Social functioning and interpersonal relating
- Physical and somatic effects
- Sexual dysfunction

Early research has been reinforced and consolidated by more recent studies (Finkelhor, 1990). There is general consensus regarding the symptom profile seen in adult female survivors of sexual abuse who did not receive treatment as children. A review of the literature on the effects of sexual abuse (Schetky, 1990) indicated that long-term sequelae of sexual abuse include the following:

- High degrees of psychiatric dysfunction and psychiatric hospitalization (overrepresentation and longer stays of adult victims of sexual abuse)

  —Depression (most studies comment on the high prevalence of these symptoms in victims of incest, with the range from 33 to 100 percent)

—Post-traumatic stress disorder and anxiety (prevalence rates close to 50 percent)
—Dissociative disorders and conversion reactions
—Personality disorders (borderline, dependent, antisocial)

- Increased substance abuse
- Self-abusive behavior (increased suicide attempts, self-mutilation) and revictimization (repeated abuse, battering prevalent in 50 percent of abused women)
- Academic and learning difficulties
- Impaired interpersonal relationships and trust (feeling detached, unable to trust, hostile)
- Impaired parenting

Three underlying negative effects may account for the range of symptoms seen in sexual abuse victims (Gelinas, 1983):

- *Chronic traumatic neurosis* may occur, manifested as intense affect, fear, cognitive incapacitation, helplessness, intrusive symptoms, use of dissociative defenses, and frequent nightmares.
- *Relational imbalances* (betrayal of trust, exploitation, and skewed family relationships) continue to occur with parts of a survivor's personality hyperdeveloped (caretaking and sense of responsibility) at the expense of other parts (self-esteem, social skills, and self-identity).
- *Increased intergenerational risk* of incest has also been associated with a history of childhood sexual abuse.

Childhood sexual abuse is clearly a far-reaching and serious problem that appears to result in long-term sequelae (Beitchman et al., 1992). Some conclusions about the long-term effects of sexual abuse can be drawn from recurrent themes in the many studies of sexual abuse. In comparison with women not reporting a history of sexual abuse, women who do report such a history more commonly show evidence of sexual dysfunction. They also report homosexual experiences in adolescence or childhood, show symptoms of anxiety and fear (which may be related to force or threat of force during the abuse), and show evidence of depression, revictimization experiences, and suicidal ideation and behavior, particularly when exposed to force. Insufficient evidence exists to show a definitive relationship between a history of childhood sexual abuse and a postsexual abuse syndrome or between childhood sexual abuse and personality disorders such as multiple personality disorder and borderline personality disorder (Beitchman et al., 1992).

IMPACT

Sgroi and Bunk (1988) and Courtois (1988) have identified a number of variables that seem to influence the impact of the sexually abusive experience on the individual. It is paramount to consider the survivor's perception of, and reaction to, variables such as:

- type of enticement/engagement strategy used,
- feared consequences of noncompliance,
- psychological importance of the relationship between the child and the abuser,
- age at onset,
- duration of the abuse,
- child's ability to accomplish developmental tasks,
- type of sexual abuse behavior,
- reaction to and events following disclosure/discovery, and
- context of the sexual abuse.

Also, when the relationship between abuse-specific variables and particular outcomes is examined, longer-lasting negative effects of sexual abuse appear to be correlated with:

- abuse by a father or a stepfather,
- use or threat of force, and
- a lack of support from a close adult.

It is highly probable that sexual activity which is intrusive (involving penetration) and of long duration is most disruptive. School-age children seem to be at greatest risk for developing behavioral problems related to the abuse, at least in short-term studies. Girls are more likely than boys to show acute distress following sexual abuse (Schetky, 1990). The relationship between age at onset of abuse and outcome remains unclear, although more evidence exists to support a more traumatic impact of postpubertal abuse than prepubertal abuse.

Healthier long-term adjustment has been found to correlate with a positive and supportive reaction of mothers (or other significant caretakers) to the disclosure of the abuse (Finkelhor, 1990). This support may provide continuity, stability, security, and a reality check for the child, which in turn further facilitates self- and social development (Cole and Putnam, 1992).

MALE SURVIVORS OF SEXUAL ABUSE

A number of studies have expanded upon previous findings to include the effect of sexual abuse on boys. Although there has been a marked similarity between symptomatic responses of boys and those of girls, some differences have been discussed in the literature. It appears that boys tend to externalize (act out aggressively, hurt others, express sexual interest in other children), while girls are more likely to act depressed (Friedrich, 1988; Urquiza and Crowley, 1986). Boys also seem to express more fears of homosexuality and of becoming perpetrators themselves (Bruckner and Johnson, 1987). Stein and colleagues (1988), in a survey of adults in Los Angeles, found that both men and women were twice as likely to have a psychiatric disorder if they had a history of sexual abuse. Women's psychopathology was more extensive, falling in the areas of affective disorders, anxiety disorders, and alcohol abuse. It has been suggested that males with a higher degree of psychopathology may be found in the prison system rather than in psychiatric hospitals (Harrison, 1998).

Cases of male adults molested as children are frequently underreported, while, in fact, it is believed that the actual number of male sexual abuse victims closely parallels that of females (Elliott and Briere, 1992; Mann, J., 1973; Mann, T., 1991; Mann, D., 1992). The minimization of male sexual abuse may result from a combination of different factors (Thomas, Nelson, and Sumners, 1994; Mendel, 1995):

- Sociological and psychological attitudes that view males as powerful, active, and competent rather than helpless, weak, and passive, a victim (the "male ethic")
- The stigma of homosexuality and the belief that sexual abuse may signify the victim is gay
- Belief in males' indiscriminate and constant sexual willingness
- Failure to recognize or ask the male client about a history of sexual abuse and the reluctance to self-disclose

Sexual victimization conjures up an image of reduced manhood, which threatens the perception of masculinity. Behaviors such as revictimization, compulsive, precocious, or aggressive sexual behaviors, chronic depression, somatic complaints, substance abuse, marital and intimacy problems, and problems with authority have been associated with unresolved childhood abuse (Mann, 1992; Allers and Benjack, 1991). Males tend to normalize the abuse more than females, express greater homophobic concerns and sexual identity confusion, and demonstrate an increased externalization of their behavior in expressions of anger and aggression.

Gartner (1997) has identified three areas of concern for male survivors of abuse. These include difficulty defining the experience as abuse rather than sexual initiation, the implications of the abuse for developing sexual and gender identities, and the effects of the abuse on forming adult intimate and sexual relations. Confusion about gender and sexual identity is a primary problem for males because the feelings of vulnerability, helplessness, and powerlessness engendered by the abuse violate the tenets of the cultural definitions of masculinity (Lisak, 1995).

Harrison (1998) discusses the unique needs of the male survivor of sexual abuse within the Euro-American culture. The existing stereotype of the male willing to fight and die before allowing himself to become a victim extends the shame associated with the trauma to include the shame of gender identity inadequacy. Most directly associated with violent crime and the misuse of power in our society, men are traditionally not viewed as victims. These socialization constraints may lead males to exhibit their distress differently. The male victim may funnel the "soft feelings" associated with victimization (sadness, vulnerability, helplessness, shame) into more congruent sex-role expressions, such as anger (Briere, 1998).

The survivor, family members, and the public often fear that the victim will become the perpetrator (Bruckner and Johnson, 1987), based on the belief that the male who has been abused may have an even stronger need to identify with the aggressor to survive. It may be that males externalize their own distress by distressing others, suggesting one factor which may contribute to victims becoming offenders (Briere, 1998). It is commonly believed that males cannot be raped or molested by women; therefore, they must have been willing participants or even perpetrators. The issue of them (perpetrators) versus us (victims) becomes confused and cloudy.

Elliott and Briere (1992) suggest that although a higher number of child molesters have been abused themselves the correlation between molestation as a child and subsequent perpetration is small. Avoiding revictimization by becoming a perpetrator may be one way a male attempts to deal with his sense of powerlessness and lack of control. Yet, the adult male is just as likely to perpetuate the cycle of repeated revictimization, or break the cycle by becoming a protector in society (Lew, 1990).

COGNITIVE EFFECTS

These findings reflect the type of reactions studied most often by researchers, that is, stress-related, affective symptoms. Distinct abuse-specific cognitive reactions are also prevalent. Incest victims think differently from nonvictims; their fundamental attitudes, beliefs, and self-conceptions and worldview have been disrupted. As a result, their construction of reality and causal attributions are often based on distorted cognitive schema (Fine, 1990). Different symptoms and responses result from the individual's unique attempts to cope with and understand the abuse.

Childhood sexual abuse has been conceptualized as a form of post-traumatic stress disorder (PTSD). Abuse survivors frequently describe intrusive and constricting PTSD symptoms, such as flashbacks, nightmares, numbing of affect, a sense of estrangement, and sleep complications. Finkelhor (1990) has broadened this conceptualization of the traumatic response to abuse from its primary focus in the affective realm to include traumatic reactions in the cognitive realm as well. "As a result of being abused, children get distorted cognitive maps about sex, family, their worth, and how to get what they need from the world" (p. 328). In addition, some victims do not display PTSD symptoms, but rather experience other problems such as depression and sexual dysfunction. Finkelhor contends that the experience of sexual abuse does not only occur under violent conditions that result in feelings of overwhelming helplessness; the trauma can also result from the internalized meaning of the event (e.g., exploitation). Distorted socialization associated with the abusive episode may affect other areas of psychological functioning as well.

Finkelhor and Browne (1985) have proposed a model of traumagenic dynamics to account for the long-term effects of sexual abuse:

- Traumatic sexualization (sexual dysfunction, preoccupation, compulsions, promiscuity, confusion regarding gender identity)
- Betrayal (difficulty assessing trustworthiness, establishing intimate relationships, setting limits and boundaries)
- Stigmatization (shame, guilt, diminished self-esteem)
- Powerlessness (lack of or need to control, learned helplessness, increased victimization, self-destructive behavior)

This model presumes that four main domains of development (sexuality, ability to trust in personal relationships, self-esteem, and sense of the ability to influence the world) may be affected, depending on the character of the abuse (Finkelhor, 1990). Different mechanisms may traumatize the child by distorting cognitive and affective capacities. The emphasis of this approach is to see the trauma of the abuse as stemming from not only the abuse but also from the conditioning process that precedes and follows it, as well as the meaning assigned to it by the individual.

This conceptualization of post-traumatic stress disorder has been further elaborated to include the effects of prolonged, repeated trauma. The term "complex post-traumatic stress disorder" has been coined to account for a spectrum of conditions that result from trauma. This spectrum ranges from a brief stress reaction to a classic case of PTSD to a complex syndrome resulting from prolonged trauma (Herman, 1992, p. 119).

COGNITIVE PROCESSES,
THE DEVELOPMENT OF A BELIEF SYSTEM,
AND SEXUAL ABUSE

Cognitions are the basis for defining and establishing patterns of relating to others. The child's understanding of internal reality (self), external reality (the environment of other people and things), and relationships between oneself and one's environment is developed through his/her *cognitive response cycle* (Sgroi and Bunk, 1988). In the cognitive response cycle, an event occurs that is understood in terms of the child's internal reality, the immediate external reality, and peripheral external messages. The child then has a cognitive response, a way of understanding and integrating the event. A psychological response follows the cognitive interpretation of the event, serving to promote the child's sense of well-being and control.

A number of researchers have hypothesized that the cognitive process of the sexually abused child results in distorted cognitions and is at the basis of the disturbances in relationships which adult survivors frequently experience (McCann and Pearlman, 1990; Sgroi and Bunk, 1988; Fine, 1990; Finkelhor, 1990). For example, when a child is sexually abused, two sources of information contribute to the child's understanding of the event. The internal processes may be any combination of conflicting emotions, such as fear, pleasure, anger, and confusion, while external information includes the abuser's behavior and messages conveyed by other sources in the child's world (respect adults, keep sexual behavior secret, etc.). The child who then begins to feel out of control, overwhelmed, and inadequate may seek ways to protect himself/herself from these feelings. Responses such as minimization of the event, denial, or dissociation serve a self-protective function and develop as the child's preferred coping mechanisms. "It is likely that the basis of any relational disturbance might be found in the individual's cognitions about himself or herself, about other people in the world in general, and about the connections between the internal and external reality" (Sgroi and Bunk, 1988, p. 179).

Similarly, certain distorted beliefs associated with the victims' sexual abuse in childhood are important sources of their mood disturbances and related problems in adulthood (Jehu, 1988). As a child, the survivor may have been confused about the thoughts and feelings he/she had about himself/herself; the survivor may also have been confused by the dissonant messages he/she received from internal and external reality. Unable to integrate the confusing messages, the survivor may have consequently developed a pattern of relating to the world that was based on confused cognitions and distorted beliefs (Sgroi and Bunk, 1988, p. 179).

A person's fundamental beliefs are likely to be invalidated by a traumatic event such as sexual abuse (Roth and Newman, 1991). For example, the world may no longer be seen as a benign, pleasurable, and rewarding place nor viewed as meaningful, predictable, controllable, and just. The self may be seen as unworthy (no longer lovable, good, and competent) and other people as untrustworthy. To assimilate this traumatic experience, the individual must modify the existing belief system. These modifications can be either adaptive or maladaptive. Adaptive, realistic coping or a chronic state of negative affect and restricted way of relating to the world may result, depending upon the individual's current situation (Roth and Newman, 1991). Judith Herman (1992) has proposed three major forms of adaptation that permit the child to survive in an environment of chronic abuse and preserve the appearance of normality:

- Elaboration of dissociative defenses
- Development of a fragmented identity
- Pathological regulation of emotional states

Beliefs and expectations (schemata) about the self and others both shape and are shaped by the person's experience in the world. Victims of sexual abuse may experience disturbances in schemata within one or more of five areas of psychological and interpersonal functioning: safety, trust, power, esteem, and intimacy (McCann et al., 1988). The relationship between life experiences, cognitive schemata (systems of meaning) and their associated emotions, and psychological functioning helps determine an individual's unique experience of the traumatic event, which in turn affects later interpersonal reactions.

These schemata develop sequentially through one's life experiences and form the organizing framework for the individual's thoughts and feelings. Beliefs may be confirmed or disconfirmed by information from the environment or from within the individual. Disruptions, or arrests in the development of these schemata, may occur, depending on the age at which the abuse happened. Depending on the person's unique system of meaning and his/her current psychological state, discrepant information may be denied or assimilated (matched with existing schemata), or the existing schemata may be changed to accommodate the discrepant input. For example, positive esteem, safety, or power schemata may be protected by one person's denial of the uncomfortable emotions or victimization memories. A second person may assimilate the experience in a way that undermines positive schemata. This person then may believe himself/herself to be bad or that others are untrustworthy. The most adaptive response may be the ability to integrate past abusive experiences by deriving new meanings and altering nonadaptive schemata in the process (McCann et al., 1988).

In assessing and treating survivors of sexual abuse, it is important to understand the development of the individual's belief system, how the beliefs were affected by the abuse experience, how they shaped the person's interpretation of that event, and how they may be contributing to problems in current functioning. This approach recognizes that survivors interpret the abuse through their own system of meaning. An assessment of their central maladaptive schemata allows an understanding of the relationship between life experiences, beliefs, feelings, and psychological functioning. The treatment for these clients can then be molded to address their specific needs (McCann et al., 1988).

Chapter 2

Treatment: Toward Integration

Current data and related research suggest effective psychotherapy for post–sexual abuse trauma should address both early victimization experiences and "here and now" concerns as well (Briere and Runtz, 1988). The victim of sexual abuse may be desensitized to memories of the trauma and may be provided with a cathartic release through relating the details of the abuse (Gelinas, 1983; Jehu, 1988). It is generally recognized that "abuse-specific" therapy is a preferred method of intervention. Such treatment entails the expression of abuse-related feelings, clarification of erroneous, distorted beliefs and negative attributions, teaching abuse-prevention skills, and diminishing stigma and isolation (Finkelhor and Berliner, 1995).

PHILOSOPHY OF TREATMENT

Treatment of sexual abuse survivors should be guided by certain philosophical values (see Table 2.1).

TABLE 2.1. Philosophy of Treatment

- Empowerment
- Recovery within relationships
- Collaboration
- Education
- Integration
- Accountability
- Pacing

- Treatment should emphasize empowerment, a belief in the individual's ability to grow and change, strength rather than weakness, connection rather than disconnection. Therapy should be directed toward restoring control to the survivor and decreasing helplessness.
- Recovery by the survivor occurs within the context of relationships, emphasizing regenerating the basic capacity for trust, autonomy, intimacy, and identity (Herman, 1992).
- The therapist does not "cure" the client but rather facilitates the integration of the abusive experience.
- Therapy is both educational and therapeutic and may differ from person to person.
- The client's psychological responses to trauma may be considered logical adaptations or accommodations to illogical circumstances. A major goal of treatment is for the client to integrate memories of the traumatic childhood experience within the framework of the adult understanding, perspective, and experience.
- Children are never considered responsible for their sexual exploitation; sexual contact between an adult and a child is always the adult's responsibility. Ethically, adult-child sex is wrong because the fundamental conditions of free and informed consent cannot prevail when the child is less powerful than the adult (Finkelhor, 1979; Briere, 1989). The adult is held accountable for the abuse; care should be taken by the therapist, however, not to scapegoat. A child's intense loyalty to his/her parents must be explicitly supported in treatment (Finkelhor, 1979; Gelinas, 1983; Mennen and Meadow, 1992).
- Therapy is paced according to the client's rhythm; the emotional intensity of the treatment may need to be modulated as memories are confronted and integrated (Briere, 1989).

TREATMENT APPROACHES

Individual Treatment

Treatment of sexual abuse has been approached from different theoretical perspectives (Courtois, 1991). One view regards abuse as a significant life trauma that results in *traumatic victimization* and PTSD symptomology. The child's negative symptoms are viewed as a natural, protective response to an abnormal life event. These symptoms may become disconnected from the original trauma. Memories and affect must be reintegrated in therapy (Finkelhor and Browne, 1985).

Sexual abuse is also believed to distort the child's frame of reference in regard to self and others. It distorts the sense of safety, trust, power, intimacy, and self-esteem. A fragmented sense of self may result in an altered system of meaning because of the distorted cognitive interpretations of the abusive experience. The *self-development constructivist* approach to treatment emphasizes strengthening the damaged, distorted sense of self through restructuring cognitive conceptions of self and assigning new meaning to the experience (McCann and Pearlman, 1990).

Sexual victimization results in multiple *loss*—loss of control, loss of safety, loss of trust, and loss of childhood. Loss theorists suggest that losses must be mourned before the client can heal (Janoff-Bulman and Frieze, 1983). Sexual abuse also represents an imbalance in power and autonomy. Treatment, from the perspective of *feminist* theorists, should be directed toward empowering the client to determine his/her own life experience (Laidlaw and Malmo, 1990). Therapy should allow alleviation of guilt and shame, relocation of the responsibility for the abuse to the offender, and venting of anger and rage. Therapy should also facilitate the development of a positive self-image and adaptive survival skills.

Recovery from sexual abuse may be limited unless psychotherapy addresses victimization as a central factor in the individual's psychopathology. The crux of clinical intervention is to help the adult survivor examine his/her own sexual victimization experiences to discover and articulate the personal perception of the meaning of the experience. It is important to address certain questions in therapy to reach this end (Sgroi and Bunk, 1988, p. 139). Therapeutic intervention addresses recurrent questions and themes that focus on the experience of the abuse as a child and the understanding of it as an adult (Sgroi and Bunk, 1988).

- *Why did I go along?* This question addresses feelings of blame, responsibility, shame, and guilt, as well as the consequences of noncompliance.

- *What really happened to me?* This uncovers the facts of the abuse to dispel additional self-questioning, such as "Am I crazy?"
- *Why did I keep the secret?* This taps into feelings of vulnerability and lack of control as the survivor questions, "Why did I let the abuse continue?"
- *What will I lose if I tell now? Am I damaged for life?* These questions reveal concerns about ever being a whole human being again. Clients will stop wondering whether they are damaged for life after they have experienced success in caring for others and being cared for by others.
- *Why is it so hard for me to stay connected to others?* This addresses survivors' perceived sense of inadequacy and failure with regard to how they relate to others.

Judith Herman (1992) suggests that recovery from psychological trauma and abuse evolves in stages. In the first stage, it is essential to establish safety and a strong therapeutic alliance. The survivor is then able to begin the tasks of reconstruction, remembering, and mourning. Finally, the survivor seeks to reconnect with everyday life and to integrate the abusive experience.

The sequencing of treatment and the choice of strategy within each treatment phase is an important consideration (Courtois, 1991). "The healing process has been viewed as traveling up a spiral, passing through the same stages again and again but at a different level, with a different perspective" (Bass and Davis, 1988, p. 59). Treatment begins with the decision to heal and a commitment to treatment. It progresses through the emergency stage; memory processing, believing it was real; recounting the abuse; resolving issues of responsibility, self-blame, and complicity; recognizing, labeling, and expressing feelings; grieving; cognitive restructuring of distorted beliefs; disclosure; confirmation; self-appreciation, self-determination, and behavior change. Treatment of adults victimized as children, therefore, helps them understand and evaluate that victimization in terms of its impact on current functioning. It involves a process of grieving for what was lost in childhood, letting go of childhood needs or expectations, and understanding the experience in terms of their adult system of meaning.

Group Treatment

Group therapy represents another and, for many, the most essential healing mode of treatment (Brandt, 1989). It requires attention to the needs and desires of others and the development of mutual supports. Yalom (1975) describes the major curative factors of group treatment. Successful group therapy imparts information, instills hope, and demonstrates the universality of experiences. It provides a corrective recapitulation of the primary family group and allows for the development of social techniques through modeling, imitation, interpersonal learning, group cohesiveness, and catharsis.

Numerous authors have written about the efficacy of group therapy for adult survivors of incest (Cole and Barney, 1987; Herman and Schatzow, 1987; Courtois and Sprei, 1988; Sgroi and Bunk, 1988; Goodwin and Talwar, 1989; Kreidler and England, 1990). Courtois and Sprei (1988) note that many of the aftereffects of child sexual abuse are likely to be resistant to therapy unless treated in a comprehensive manner.

Individual therapy initially can benefit most victims of trauma by allowing the development of a safe and trusting relationship in which to disclose the trauma, express, explore, and validate emotions and experiences, and teach affect regulation. However, this kind of relationship as the sole mode of treatment is limited. It is difficult to fully resolve issues of secrecy, shame, and stigma in individual treatment alone. An alliance of secrecy and dependency may be reinforced in individual therapy, inhibiting growth at later stages (Herman and Schatzow, 1984). "When individual treatment is complemented with group therapy, clients more readily accept the multidimensional impact of the incestuous events by weakening the alliance of secrecy through open sharing with others who suffer common conflicts" (Drews and Bradley, 1989, p. 58).

Although individual therapy is an important component in the treatment of sexual abuse and trauma, it cannot address all the dimensions necessary for healing. Participation in a psychotherapeutic and psychoeducational group should be included as an essential element in any treatment program.

> Although no controlled studies exist, group therapy is regarded as the treatment of choice for many patients with PTSD (among

them, survivors of incest), either as the sole form of therapy, or as an adjunct to individual psychotherapy . . . the unique therapeutic virtue of the group is the opportunity it provides to experience, explore and work through interpersonal relationships. . . . Group psychotherapy reestablishes a peer group in which sharing and reliving of common experiences may facilitate entrance into a world of adult relationships where others can be regarded as both subjects and objects. (van der Kolk, 1987b, pp. 164, 166, and 167)

Group treatment can offer therapeutic benefit beyond that of individual therapy because it broadens the counseling experience and demonstrates that sexual abuse is an experience not unique to the individual (Bruckner and Johnson, 1987). As an addition to individual treatment, it allows the survivor to work with others experiencing similar pain and struggles, reduces isolation, and provides caring support in a safe environment. Victims can use the group experience as a means of examining feelings, learning to trust, and establishing healthy relationships.

Group therapy can validate the reality of the victimization, allow the survivor to build self esteem, and confirm affective experiences that often are denied or distorted by the survivor and others in his/her family (Cole and Barney, 1987; Kreidler and England, 1990). Issues of guilt, shame, stigma, and isolation may be more fully resolved in the group. Survivors need to understand the basis for the confusion, powerlessness, anger, and sense of being overwhelmed and out of control in the context of also knowing, through experience, that they are capable of different, more functional, less costly, and less destructive responses to problems in their current lives. "To be effective, treatment for the adult survivor must include opportunities to practice more functional and effective responses and coping mechanisms" (Sgroi and Bunk, 1988, p. 160). Peer group therapy provides a forum to practice new behaviors, work through family dynamics, and explore current interpersonal relationships (Bruckner and Johnson, 1987; Agosta and Loring, 1988). Autonomy, responsibility, diversity, and control are fostered as the group serves to empower its members. Self-responsibility and self-care are emphasized.

Group treatment is also an important medium for addressing the relational disturbances associated with sexual abuse. Sgroi and Bunk (1988) contend that:

> Group psychotherapy is the treatment modality of choice for adult survivors of sexual abuse who present primarily with relational disturbances. Long-term individual therapy is an inefficient and ineffective method of repairing the relational disruption. . . . This may be associated with the one on one aspect of individual treatment, or more specifically, with the intense, isolated and somewhat secretive nature of the format. . . . The adult survivor's experience of uniqueness or of being different from everyone else in the world is another important factor in the recommendation for group therapy. . . . In a therapy group, the survivor learns for herself that other people have had similar experiences. . . . In group therapy, the adult survivor has the opportunity to relearn the rules of relationships with all the other group members. . . . Group members can practice being direct, honest, and caring with each other within the group therapy sessions. We have found this to be the most effective method of counteracting the relational disturbances introduced during the childhood experience of sexual abuse. (p. 185)

Group treatment can therefore be viewed as a complement to the intensive, individual exploration of the trauma. It is a primary mode in which to address the interpersonal, relational aspects of the abuse.

Group therapy is not, however, without its limitations. Briere (1998) suggests that group treatment may be potentially harmful to participants who have insufficient degrees of affect regulation. It may be these individuals who end up dropping out of the group prematurely because of their inability to tolerate the intense affect expressed in the group. For this reason, it may be necessary to screen and match potential members for affect-regulation capacity prior to group participation and provide pretraining in affect regulation when necessary.

EFFICACY OF GROUP TREATMENT

Few systematic evaluations of treatment outcome in group therapy for survivors of sexual abuse have been conducted. Consumer evaluations (self-reports) have been used to evaluate group therapy programs for this population (Herman and Schatzow, 1984). These evaluations indicate that the most consistent change reported is increased self-esteem, while the most helpful aspect of therapy was the sharing of feelings with those who understand. Positive outcomes were generally confined to improvements in self-concept, while relationships with others, work, and sexuality did not show consistent improvement (Herman and Schatzow, 1984; Cahill et al., 1991).

Alexander and colleagues (1991) conducted one of the few controlled outcome studies comparing the effectiveness of two different models of group therapy for survivors of sexual abuse with a control condition. A process group format was compared with an interpersonal transaction group format and a wait-list control group. When compared with the wait-list control, both group formats were more effective in improving adjustment and did not differ significantly from each other. Results from this study suggest that short-term group therapy is a viable and effective means of intervention in reducing depression and distress and in promoting social adjustment. It is suggested that a combination of the two formats may be the ideal framework for maximizing the beneficial effects of each. Alexander and her associates stress the benefits of the group milieu to practice newly acquired skills such as achieving intimacy, asserting one's own needs, and resolving conflict. The group setting may provide an environment that more closely resembles natural settings outside the therapy framework, thereby facilitating the generalization of the newly learned skills (Alexander, Neimeyer, and Follette, 1991, p. 228).

MODELS OF GROUP TREATMENT

Long-Term Groups

Different models have been suggested for group treatment. A *long-term, open-ended group* has been recommended for this population because of the need for in-depth reworking of the core issues of sexual abuse. The long-term group allows more time for this in-depth exploration of issues that is necessary for resolution of chronic symptoms. Group cohesiveness, which develops over time, allows for greater risk taking, interpersonal learning, and retrieval of memories. Also, group members at different stages of treatment provide models for other group members to observe; senior members can share their experiences with newer members (remembering the one caveat with regard to affect-regulation capacity). A practical consideration, the need for a waiting list, may be avoided, as placement in a long-term, ongoing group can be immediate (Blake-White and Kline, 1985; Goodwin and Talwar, 1989; Mennen and Meadow, 1992).

Donaldson and Cordes-Green (1994) present an example of a long-term treatment program designed to provide a change-oriented therapy in a supportive context. Clients participate, on the average, for one year. The program evolves in stages, including five sessions of individual therapy, a four-session educational group, three to four pretherapy group orientation sessions, and a six-month therapy group. According to these authors, the program attempts to meet a wide range of needs, while allowing individual choices. A shorter group was considered insufficient to accomplish this goal or deal with topics such as family systems issues, individual developmental processes, grief, and assertion.

Self-Help Groups

Self-help groups, such as Survivors of Incest Anonymous, have also become quite prevalent. Such groups, although not appropriate for all sexual abuse survivors, are felt to "foster a sense of health and competence. They may offer a safer and more therapeutic environment than the available professional services . . . [and] develop a social analysis of personal problems and sometimes offer the opportunity for collective action" (Herman and Hirschman, 1981, p. 197, as cited in Cahill et al., 1991).

Goodwin and Talwar (1989) differentiate between self-help and therapist-led groups. Self-help groups for victims include many of the same aspects as therapist-led groups, focusing on decreasing shame and guilt, while increasing interpersonal support and coping strategies. Therapist-led groups, however, tend to focus more on processing and interpreting the meaning of memories of the abuse. Directed self-help mutual support groups are seen as useful adjunct resources for the treatment of various populations victimized by sexual abuse (Hall, Kassees, and Hoffman, 1986).

Short-Term, Time-Limited Group Therapy

The majority of the clinical literature recommends a *short-term, time-limited, group treatment* approach for survivors of sexual abuse (Cahill et al., 1991). The time-limited, goal-directed group seems to be appropriate for survivors of sexual abuse, providing both focus and safety. (This is in contrast to the open-ended group, which may be a less appropriate, less safe environment for uncovering the trauma of the abuse.) The structured format keeps the focus on sexual abuse, provides structure for dealing with difficult emotions, and facilitates bonding between group members, while still establishing distinct boundaries and expectations (Herman and Schatzow, 1984; Alexander and Follette, 1987; Herman, 1992). Clearly defined boundaries limit the consequences of pain and regression that inevitably accompany the working through of trauma.

Due to its short-term nature, this model also highlights impending loss and separation, while it promotes the strengths and control of the members. The defined termination provides the opportunity to rework grief over previous losses of support and nurturance: "In many ways, short-term, time-limited group therapy provides a group experience for incest victims which is antithetical to that which they experienced in their incestuous family of origin" (Cahill et al., 1991, p. 117).

The time-limited, structured approach allows the integration of educationally based and therapeutic interventions. It can provide for teaching and modeling of behaviors and skills that effect change toward more functional relationship patterns and decision-making processes (Drews and Bradley, 1989).

The short-term, psychoeducational format is valuable in defining common issues for this population. The time limit and structure allow the development of trust and safety, yet they do restrict the depth of resolution of the issues that are introduced and limit the degree of integration of the past abusive experiences with the individual's current functioning. Once safety and a greater degree of intimacy have been established within the highly structured group, it may be valuable to allow time for less structured interactions, determined by the needs of the group members themselves.

Caution is necessary when promoting disclosure of sexual abuse trauma in a group format. As Briere (1998) suggests, the group format may be less amenable than individual treatment to containing the anxiety associated with disclosure and memory retrieval. Although the group has great potential to heal, management of possible harmful effects may become more difficult. Lasting negative consequences may occur when the design of the group does not provide clear expectations or adequate internal and external supports (Galinsky and Schopler, 1977).

It is essential to use the beneficial aspects inherent in group treatment and to facilitate resolution and mastery of the trauma of sexual abuse, while ensuring safeguards against the risk. Using a "therapeutic window" and specific protective techniques, such as appropriate screening (especially concerning affect regulation), normative expectations, grounding, and cognitive restructuring, has been recommended (Cole and Barney, 1987). The concept of a "therapeutic window" refers to a phase between the extremes of denial and intrusion of posttraumatic symptoms during which resolution can progress. The therapist is able to time and pace interventions to ease the distress associated with reworking the trauma.

The short-term, time-limited, psychoeducational group is designed to minimize regression and emphasize the strengths of the individual. Goals include decreasing feelings of shame and guilt, facilitating members' identification with others who have shared similar experiences, and helping members develop new ways of handling situations that elicit feelings about the incest. The group may help members take an active stance in confronting the offender, if desired, rebalance relationships within the family, and establish an awareness of risk factors to prevent further abuse (Herman and Schatzow, 1984; Webb and Leehan, 1996).

GROUP ORGANIZATION AND STRUCTURE

Certain aspects of group organization and structure have been discussed in the literature. These include the role and gender of the therapists, duration and number of sessions, and selection of members, themes, goals, process, and stages of group development.

Most groups use cotherapists, sometimes of the same gender as group members, other times using female-male dyads to re-create a surrogate family. This encourages transference toward both male and female authority figures. It is generally believed, however, that same-sex therapists (as each other and as group members) provide an environment which better allows a decrease in defensiveness and a more natural exploration of sex-role stereotypes and expectations. Regardless of gender, the relationship between the therapists is key to the establishment of a safe, supportive, and cohesive group (Goodwin and Talwar, 1989).

Although twelve treatment sessions are considered by some to be the minimal time required for "a series of dynamic events to develop, flourish and be available for discussion, examination and resolution" (Mann, 1973, p. 15), the duration of short-term, time-limited groups has ranged from ten to twenty-four sessions. The pressure of a time limit facilitates bonding and diminishes resistance to sharing, offers a structure to contain regressive aspects of treatment, and permits focus on the theme of incest (Herman and Schatzow, 1984).

A group of six to eight members is recommended as the optimal size. Members should be able to use therapy to help them integrate their understanding of the sexual abuse with their current behavior and not be further traumatized by the therapy itself. In addition, these participants should have fairly stable life situations (no new changes in relationships, employment, residence, etc.) and should not be actively suicidal or psychotic. The individual who will benefit most from these groups is "psychologically minded, in individual treatment prior to the group, involved in a relationship with at least one significant individual and is having some success in work or school" (Goodman and Nowack-Scibelli, 1985, p. 541). Prospective members should express motivation and positive expectations about participation, be functioning reasonably well in day-to-day life, and have an ongoing relationship with an individual therapist (Herman and Schatzow, 1984).

The group typically develops in stages. Initially, it is directed toward the development of a trusting and safe environment in which to explore the abuse. Ground rules are specified, and goals are generated. The focus then moves on to the details of incest, including disclosure of specifics of the experience, an exploration of the feelings, and the connection of these feelings with memories of the experience. Past and current relationships are examined within the context of the group interactions. New skills are taught and practiced. The group ends with the termination directed toward the resolution of feelings of abandonment and loss.

THEMES

Major recurrent themes are commonly addressed in the group. These include, but are not limited to, trust, intimacy and sexual difficulties, identity issues, current emotional distress, low self-esteem, management of pathology, interpersonal relationships, potential for abusing, revictimization, physical symptoms, drug and alcohol abuse, and professional difficulties.

Coker (1990) suggests that breaking the silence (disclosure) must be included as an integral component of any group program, when a sufficient sense of safety in the group has been established. Disclosure allows movement beyond a pattern of guilt, shame, secrecy, and suppression. As mentioned, safety and trust, blame and guilt are central themes in incest therapy. Survivors can begin to assign new meaning to the dynamics of guilt as they gain an understanding that they were not to blame.

Identification of maladaptive coping strategies and the development of new and effective means of coping is another key component of group programs. Awakening senses and feelings, integrating those feelings with the memories of the abuse, and processing memories are important to the resolution of the trauma associated with the abuse. A discussion of sexuality is necessary in any group, as it is one area that has been directly affected by the abuse. Recognition of their own needs, feelings, and emotions and mourning the losses of childhood also facilitate the survivor's recovery. A life inventory, individual needs and self-esteem assessment, goal planning, and teaching strategies for self-nurturing (self-care and self-support) may be important interventions to use with survivors to help them move forward (Courtois, 1988; Herman and Schatzow, 1987; Hays, 1985; Tharinger, 1990).

Another theme central in the treatment of incest survivors is the understanding and modification of the process of victimization. The process of victimization involves the development of negative assumptions, attributions, and self-perceptions in survivors of sexual abuse. Guilt, low self-esteem, self-blame, underestimation of self-efficacy and self-worth, and learned helplessness are common cognitive sequelae to the abuse. "Effective psychotherapy of abuse trauma must include interventions to help the survivor update his/her victimization-related assumptions. The client is taught to recognize and alter abuse-distorted thoughts, beliefs, and perceptions through cognitive restructuring [helping clients become aware of their distorted beliefs and developing accurate alternatives]" (Jehu, 1988, cited in Briere, 1992, p. 123).

Memory processing is often emphasized in most therapeutic groups. Different strategies have been suggested to facilitate interpretation and integration of the memories of childhood abuse. These include scheduled disclosure sessions, an insistence on remembering and verbalizing the trauma, drawing, psychodrama, writing, modeling disclosure, photographs, floor plans, and an ongoing exploration of the meaning of the experience to the individual (Goodwin and Talwar, 1989).

Chew (1998) offers an example of healing through group work. This step-by-step guide serves as a model for professionals working with this population. The thirteen-session model addresses the major concerns identified in the literature, including the development of safety, boundary setting, strength building, and consolidating a sense of self within and outside of relationships.

MALES IN GROUPS

It is believed that "men learn best about being men from other men" (Hunter, 1990, p. 137). " In all-male group situations, each man is forced to be in the company of men" (Gartner, 1997, p. 382), to confront related transferences directly, and to recognize the pressures and limitations of current models of masculinity.

Male survivors of childhood sexual abuse may have difficulty in seeking and locating treatment due to social stigma and a lack of known resources for the male population (Singer, 1989). Although group therapy has been found to be as effective for males as it is for females, it is often difficult to identify prospective male participants for groups. Harrison and Morris (1995) suggest that clinicians may unwittingly collude with the silence and become protective of their male clients. Therapists should be encouraged to refer male clients to the appropriate treatment resources.

Suggested structure and format of the group therapy program for males is similar to that described for female groups (Bruckner and Johnson, 1987; Singer, 1989; Thomas, Nelson, and Sumners, 1994). Harrison and Morris (1995) offer a treatment model specifically for male survivors, based on the premise that the modalities for facilitating treatment for males may differ from the traditional "talk" therapy model. Their model is intended to help men develop language to describe their experiences and emotions, develop healthier masculine identities and coping strategies, gain mastery over the degree of self-disclosure they make about themselves and the abuse, and integrate this history into their identities. As Mendel (1995) states, "the overarching goal in working with male survivors of childhood sexual abuse is to help them integrate their masculinity, their sense of themselves as men, with their experience of victimization" (p. 213).

The consensus is that this population is best served in same-sex groups, at least in the early stages of treatment. Both genders initially are confronting issues of them versus us, perpetrators versus victims, and male versus female, and they may find it difficult to explore issues of vulnerability, powerlessness, and lack of control in mixed-gender groups. It may be helpful to view the sequences of treatment as a process of reintegration, beginning with individual therapy, progressing to sexual abuse–specific, same-gender and then mixed-gender groups, and finally culminating in a general psychotherapy group. As individuals reintegrate their identities, they are gradually reintroduced into normalized interpersonal interactions.

SUMMARY

It is clear that childhood sexual abuse constitutes an enduring problem that may have significant ramifications for long-term development and psychosocial functioning. Victims of sexual abuse as children may experience disturbances in schemata (beliefs and expectations) within different areas of psychological and interpersonal functioning. These effects are dependent, in large part, on how the survivor assigns meaning to the traumatic event. Recovery from childhood sexual abuse is facilitated by addressing the beliefs associated with victimization as central factors in the individual's psychopathology.

Clinical intervention is designed to help the adult survivor examine his/her own sexual victimization experiences to discover and articulate the personal perception of the meaning of the experience. Individual therapy initially benefits most victims of trauma by allowing for the development of a safe and trusting relationship in which to disclose the trauma and express, explore, and validate emotions and experiences. However, there are limits to this kind of relationship as the sole mode of treatment. When individual treatment is complemented with group therapy, the alliance of secrecy is weakened. Open sharing with others who suffer common conflicts, and the multidimensional impact of the incestuous events, is more readily accepted by survivors. A short-term, psychoeducational group format has been found to be particularly effective in addressing the aftereffects of sexual abuse.

Chapter 3

Assessing Prerequisites

IDENTIFYING THE NEEDS OF THE COMMUNITY

The majority of controlled studies of survivors of sexual abuse clearly identify consistent psychosocial problems for this population. Alpert (1990) noted, however, that there is "relatively little formal education and training in child sexual abuse" (p. 324). In a national survey of psychologists' evaluation of training and competence in the areas of sexual and physical abuse, Pope and Feldman-Summers (1992) also found that those surveyed gave low ratings to their graduate training in these areas. The question arises as to how professionals are to acquire a sound knowledge base and practical expertise in the area of sexual abuse and its treatment if it is not included as part of their overall training program.

Specifically, training in the group treatment of survivors of sexual abuse is not included in most graduate programs. Although a review of the literature supports the efficacy of group treatment for this population, few detailed, step-by-step, and specific programs using established therapeutic techniques have been developed to assist professionals interested in developing a program to address the needs of this adult population. It is apparent that practitioners must address this issue and determine how they will acquire the knowledge necessary if they are to responsibly treat this clinical population. Alpert (1990) argues that it may be extremely difficult for trainees to integrate an understanding of intervention strategies and principles of planned change with the realities of dealing with a specific population and culture when developing their own programs.

The theoretically based curriculum presented here is designed to fill that gap. In addition to providing a firm basis for working with sexual abuse survivors, it also serves as a tool to be used in training new psychotherapists, as well as for assessing the reliability and skillfulness of this therapeutic practice.

Assessing Client Needs

Effective programming requires prioritizing the concerns specifically identified by the survivors of childhood sexual abuse. Based, in part, on a compilation of generic needs identified in the literature, and by key informants in the field, this process facilitates the link between the nature of the problem and its theories of treatment. It is equally important to identify distinctive themes raised by the attendant group members, thereby facilitating the direct link between their manifestation of the sequelae of the abuse and treatment.

This program was developed with these considerations in mind and, in fact, was originally created in 1992 at the request of a local citizen, to meet the specific needs of women in our community. It is highly recommended that, prior to beginning a group for survivors, an updated needs assessment be conducted. This is to ensure that treatment remains current with the state of knowledge and also to allow the program to be customized to address the specific issues of concern for that group. It would also be useful to conduct a pre and postassessment of the client's attitudes and beliefs to assess the efficacy of treatment. Various instruments can be used for this purpose, including the needs assessment included in this book, the Trauma Symptom Inventory (Briere et al., 1995), the Impact of Events Scale (Briere and Elliot, 1998), or similar inventories.

A *problem-solving process* was employed to facilitate program development (see Table 3.1). This process involves clarifying, assessing, and analyzing the nature of the problem, developing a program to address the problem, and finally, evaluating the effectiveness of the intervention.

Problem Identification and Analysis

In these stages of the problem-solving process (Maher and Bennett, 1984), a needs assessment procedure was used to clarify the problem being addressed and to provide a foundation for the proposed program. This process began in 1992 and continued throughout the

TABLE 3.1. Problem-Solving Approach to Program Development

1. Problem Identification: operationally defining problem to be addressed by program.
2. Problem Analysis: breakdown of components of problem into workable units.
3. Program Development: design and implementation of program.
4. Program Evaluation: evaluating goal attainment and satisfaction.

Source: Adapted from Maher and Bennett, 1984.

development of the program. Initial needs were defined based on a review of relevant literature. A questionnaire was then developed and sent to mental health professionals with experience in the field of psychotherapeutic treatment, and more specifically, in the area of sexual abuse treatment. Sixty-seven professional psychologists and fourteen subject matter experts were asked to identify and rate the importance of the therapeutic needs of survivors of sexual abuse, based on their professional experience. Ten survivors of sexual abuse were provided with a similar questionnaire and were asked to respond based upon their personal experiences. Current, or pretreatment, status of survivors of abuse was compared to desired, or long-term posttreatment, goals. This allowed for the prioritization of their concerns in developing and compiling the curriculum. Examples of these questionnaires are included in Appendix A.

In this sample, female professionals completed 51 percent of the questionnaires, and males completed 49 percent. Respondents ranged in age from thirty-one to sixty; a majority were Caucasian, with the remaining 5 percent representing African-American and Hispanic psychologists. Over 50 percent of the respondents were licensed after 1980, and 52 percent were employed in a private setting. Survivors of sexual abuse represented less than 10 percent of the clientele treated by 62 percent of this sample.

All survivors of sexual abuse were female and between the ages of twenty-one and forty-nine. Nine of the women were Caucasians; one was African American. Mean educational level was 3.8 years undergraduate education. All but one woman had at least one year of college education; three had obtained their master's degrees.

Previous experience in therapy ranged from two months to thirteen years, with a mean of 6.5 years. Of the women, 60 percent worked in white-collar professions and were, or previously had been, married, with at least one child. It is important to note that the demographic characteristics of this sample may differ from that of the targeted group. A local needs assessment may therefore identify additional issues that will need to be addressed in the group.

In the needs assessment survey, professionals identified what they considered the five most important issues to include in a treatment program for survivors of sexual abuse. Family-of-origin work (62 percent), exploring relationships (57 percent), cognitive restructuring (47 percent), and exploring sexuality (45 percent) were the most frequently cited elements for inclusion. Memory retrieval (38 percent), assertiveness training (25 percent), development of coping skills (29 percent), abreaction (26 percent), and providing the opportunity to interact with fellow survivors (28 percent) were also considered important components to include when treating survivors of sexual abuse.

Survivors themselves regarded trust in their own intuition and perception (57 percent), recognition and expression of their feelings (52 percent), and recognition of, and caring for, personal needs (52 percent) as the most important factors to address in treatment. The ability to trust in others (44 percent), recognize their strengths (30 percent), and establish and maintain intimate personal relationships (26 percent) were also noted as important characteristics to acquire. Survivors recognize that they have great difficulty taking care of their own needs, as well as trusting in others. It appears that trusting others is less critical to them than trusting their own perceptions and intuitions and learning to take better care of their own personal needs.

Affective, social, and cognitive domain variables identified from the literature and the needs assessment survey were used as the basis for this program design (see Table 3.2). In the affective domain, a need to recognize feelings (e.g., anger, guilt, blame, hopelessness, powerlessness, and sadness) and to be aware of needs for control, nurturance, and self-esteem were considered essential factors to be addressed in a group program. The development of trust, establishing more effective interpersonal relations, and increasing

TABLE 3.2. Programmatic Themes Identified in Needs Assessment

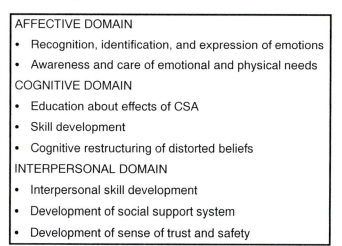

AFFECTIVE DOMAIN

- Recognition, identification, and expression of emotions
- Awareness and care of emotional and physical needs

COGNITIVE DOMAIN

- Education about effects of CSA
- Skill development
- Cognitive restructuring of distorted beliefs

INTERPERSONAL DOMAIN

- Interpersonal skill development
- Development of social support system
- Development of sense of trust and safety

social supports were the salient factors identified in the social domain. Cognitive variables included the need to obtain information about, and to understand the dynamics of, sexual abuse, family relationships, and sexuality, as well as the need to develop a more adaptive repertoire of skills (e.g., coping, assertiveness, and problem-solving skills).

PILOT PROGRAM

In the initial stages of its development, the group on which this program is based was conducted over a ten-week period. This was later increased to fifteen weeks to allow more time for a deeper exploration of the issues and to reinforce the interpersonal interactions within the group. A total of five cycles of the time-limited program were conducted over a two-year period, with the details being revised and refined. Twenty-five women, ranging in age from twenty-one to forty-nine, participated in the groups during this period. Three women dropped out during these five cycles. One woman was hospitalized after the first session due to the presentation of psychotic symptoms. A second woman, seen in individual therapy for severe anxiety and panic, could not tolerate the affect generated by the group discussions. The third woman also could not tolerate the affect, particularly after the death of her father. All these women left the group by the third session.

Although it was decided to limit our group to women to meet the expressed demands of the community, this model may be adapted for use with the male survivor. It is not recommended for mixed-gender groups, as these groups ideally should represent a later stage of treatment. Pertinent treatment issues may vary, depending on the gender distribution of the group. (Please refer to the section "Male Survivors of Sexual Abuse," in Chapter 1 for further information on gender-specific issues.) For example, gender socialization is an issue that must be addressed with both sexes. Female gender social-ization may influence women's capacity to express anger, while male gender socialization may affect men's capacity to express emotions. Again, the general consensus is that this population is best served in same-sex groups.

CONTEXT ASSESSMENT

To adapt the program to a specific target population, it is impor-tant to identify the particular issues germane to that subpopulation. For this purpose, it is useful to conduct a *context assessment*. This assessment identifies key variables that may affect the development of a particular group within a specific system. The basic parameters of the organization and the target population are thereby identified and addressed. The following is an example of a context assessment conducted for this program.

Organization

This group psychotherapy program for adult survivors of child-hood sexual abuse is designed to be implemented by professionals in private or public settings. It also may be useful as a model curriculum for training new clinicians to work with this population.

Target Population

The target population of this program is women or men, twenty-one years of age or older, who report involvement in incestuous and sexually abusive relationships during childhood, who are currently involved in individual psychotherapy, and who are not actively psychotic, suicidal, or substance abusing. Optimal group size is five to eight participants. These criteria should be determined by the specific needs of the community.

Inclusion Criterion

An incestuous and sexually abusive relationship will be defined as any sexual behaviors with minor children, whether wanted or unwanted, which occurred when there was a power differential or significant age difference between the persons involved (Sgroi, 1988). Sexual contact includes behaviors ranging from intercourse with or without consent, and all forms of penetration (oral, anal, or vaginal), to molestation (fondling), exposure, and child pornography. Sexually abusive behavior may involve a single, discrete act or multiple acts of sexual violation over time, during which the child was unable to provide informed consent. It may or may not have involved some form of coercion.

RELEVANT CONTEXT

The AVICTORY (Ability, Value, Idea, Circumstances, Timing, Obligation, Resistance, and Yield) acronym (Maher and Bennett, 1984) has been useful for evaluating relevant contextual issues associated with program development and implementation. This structure helps determine if the context in which the program is to be conducted facilitates its success and meets the needs of the target population (see Table 3.3). As an example of this assessment model, relevant contextual variables have been identified for this specific program.

Ability

Is the context able to support implementation of the program? For example, the group was originally conducted within a university training clinic and was intended to provide training experiences for doctoral students in psychology. The students provided therapy to a wide range of clients as part of their course of study. In this

TABLE 3.3. AVICTORY Model for Evaluating Context for Program Development

Ability	Is the context able to support program implementation?
Value	Will this program be a valuable addition to the services already provided?
Idea	Why form a group for survivors of childhood sexual abuse?
Circumstances	Is the environment suitable for conducting the group?
Timing	Is the timing appropriate for conducting the group?
Obligation	What is the professional obligation to treat this problem?
Resistance	What resistance to the program can be expected or anticipated?
Yield	What benefits can be gained from this program?

Source: Adapted from Maher and Bennett, 1984.

context, the graduate students served as a resource in meeting the needs of the target population. In addition, the clinic provided support in the form of coordinators, a secretary, and a business office staff who were available to act as liaison between the client and clinicians.

Using the clinic as the base for the execution of this program guaranteed the use of its facilities and equipment. It was easily accessible, and during the evening hours, parking was abundant. Therapy rooms and video equipment were available for the clinicians' use. Although the rooms were not spacious, they were adequate for the purposes of this project.

A time-limited structure was used in the execution of this program. The fifteen-session program did not attempt to resolve all the issues and problems surrounding the sexual abuse experience but was intended to provide a structured, safe environment to be used as a springboard for future therapeutic work. The shorter commitment is easier for members to make when first embarking on this endeavor and promotes more goal-oriented work. The time limit also fit in with the university's semester schedule and organizational structure of the clinic.

Value

Would this program be a valuable addition to the services already provided? The subject of sexual abuse is becoming well known and more openly talked about in today's society. More and more therapists are treating clients who report having been abused during childhood and adolescence. Secrecy has surrounded these clients in the past. Shame, guilt, and distrust may have resulted in the treatment of psychological dysfunction that was secondary to the incestuous experience (e.g., substance abuse, multiple personality disorder, borderline personality disorder). Greater recognition of the prevalence and effects of sexual abuse has led to a greater interest in, and commitment to, meeting the needs of this population. Group therapy is recommended as the treatment of choice. In addition, training in this area is seen as a high priority and, therefore, is highly valued.

Idea

Why form a group for survivors of childhood sexual abuse? "Help" for this population includes providing the opportunity for the target population to identify with others who have similar experiences and who share many of the same problems. This allows the individual to externalize the problems and recognize the abuse as the cause of the problem, not an internal personal characteristic. The group experience is an essential component of this process. Many clients have received individual therapy or group therapy for other problems, with no acknowledgement of the sexually abusive experience. This target population has been particularly underserved in the past. Individual therapy is also considered a necessary component to provide support for the client during this stressful period, to monitor the effects of the group sessions on the individual member, and to deal specifically with the impact of the group sessions on the individual.

Circumstances

Is the environment appropriate for conducting the group? When conducting any group, the physical environment should be adequate to comfortably accommodate the size of the group. With survivors

of sexual abuse, it is equally important that the emotional environment be appropriate for conducting the group. Issues of trust and
safety must be addressed directly and not just assumed to be appropriate.

Timing

*Is the timing appropriate for conducting a group? Is the orga-
nization/practice stable and committed to the treatment of survivors
of sexual abuse?* Conducting a group demands a commitment from
the therapist that may extend over a prolonged time period. The
organization or individual professional must determine if that commitment is possible. In addition, timing refers to the client's readiness to participate in a group program. Cole and Barney (1987)
discuss the concept of the therapeutic window when treating survivors of sexual abuse. This window captures the point in an individual's treatment at which the client feels safe enough to "break the
silence" to others.

Obligation

What is the professional obligation to treat this population? In
the past, the incidence of sexual abuse was thought to be rare.
Today, the mental health profession recognizes that the prevalence
of intrafamilial sexual abuse is much greater. The aftereffects of the
abusive experience were rarely addressed in therapy. It is recognized that to meet the needs of this target population today, treatment must specifically address these issues.

Resistance

What resistance to the program can be expected or anticipated?
Denial, secrecy, shame, and guilt surround the incestuous experience. Incest is taboo in most cultures and carries with it a stigma
that is reinforced societally and within the family. Freud's change
from the seduction to the oedipal theory may have actually been a
denial of the scope of the problem of incest and the reality of
women's experience. Due to this taboo, the needs of this population

may have been ignored or discounted in the past, by the public and professionals alike. Current awareness within the profession has served to greatly reduce the resistance to treatment specifically addressing sexual abuse. The target population may also be resistant to joining a group because of the nature of the problem itself. It may be too difficult for some of the potential clients to overcome the stigma and disclose their involvement in a sexually abusive relationship.

Yield

What benefits can be gained from this program? A program serving women who have been involved in an incestuous, sexually abusive relationship will serve to benefit all who are involved. The target population will be helped to break the secrecy and decrease the feelings of guilt, blame, and shame surrounding the incestuous experience. There will be a concomitant decrease in the sense of isolation, a recognition of the commonality of the experience, the development of a support network, and an increase in self-esteem and -confidence. Beginning therapists can benefit by gaining important professional experience and training in group therapy and increased knowledge of this population. Such skill development will contribute to the clinicians' competence and confidence as budding professional psychologists.

SUMMARY

This program is designed to meet the needs of women or men who have been involved in an incestuous or sexually abusive experience during childhood. The target population has been defined as individuals twenty-one years of age or older (or as determined by the need in the community). Participants should have at least one memory of the experience and be currently involved in individual psychotherapy. Ideally, each program group will encompass five to eight target population members. It is essential to determine if sufficient resources (staff, facilities, funding, time, supervised training) are available to address their needs and if the service is valued and supported within the organizational unit.

Chapter 4

The Framework

This chapter, which presents the design or framework of the program, is based upon a synthesis of elements from the review of the literature and the information obtained during the problem clarification phase of program development (i.e., identifying the needs of the population). Identifying the explicit concerns of the group members allows the program to be customized with greater flexibility. Program components, the specific structure and content of each session, and program implementation concerns will be outlined and addressed in this chapter.

INTENT

The purpose of this group psychotherapy program is to provide adult survivors of childhood sexual abuse with a forum to therapeutically explore the impact of the past trauma. The program enables persons who have been involved in sexually abusive and incestuous relationships as children and who meet certain requirements to participate in a theme-oriented, psychoeducational group. The program is geared toward persons who are twenty-one years of age or older, currently receiving individual psychotherapy, and not actively suicidal, substance abusing, or psychotic. The group is designed around a fifteen-week, time-limited structure and includes didactic presentations by the facilitators and discussion of issues raised by the group members that are pertinent to their experiences. Through the presentations, group discussions, and facilitation of group processes, group members learn to recognize and express their emotions, recognize and act upon their personal needs, acquire information about sexual abuse, and develop skills necessary for healthier human functioning.

GOALS

General goals of the group program will be presented here. More specific goals and objectives will be detailed for each group session in Chapter 6.

- Survivors of sexual abuse will experience positive interpersonal interactions by participating in weekly group discussion and by receiving supportive feedback from other participants. Participants will evaluate this experience by completing a self-report evaluation questionnaire after each session, at the end of the fifteen-week period, and three months following the completion of the program (see Appendixes C and D).
- Group members will evaluate mechanisms used in coping with the effects of abuse through weekly theme-focused group discussions. Members' understanding of these mechanisms is measured through completion of an evaluation questionnaire at the end of each session, after week fifteen of the program, and at three months following completion of the program.
- Through weekly group discussions and didactic presentations, participants will learn to recognize their personal, emotional, and physical needs and to develop strategies that they can use to care for those needs. Their ability to recognize and care for their personal needs will be measured in a self-report evaluation at the end of each session, after week fifteen of the program, and at three months following the completion of the program.
- Survivors of sexual abuse will reduce the trauma, secrecy, and taboo surrounding their abusive experience, evidenced by the participant successfully recounting some portion (amount to be determined by survivor) of their experience to the group during the fourth meeting. Opportunities for further elaboration will be provided throughout the remainder of the group sessions.
- Survivors of sexual abuse will acquire knowledge about incest trauma. At the end of each session, after week fifteen, and three months following the completion of the program, participants will complete a questionnaire evaluating the extent their knowledge of this subject area has increased.

EVALUATING THE ALTERNATIVES

Prior to adopting this short-term, time-limited model, it is important to evaluate program alternatives. A group therapy program for survivors of childhood sexual abuse may take a variety of forms. Most common among these are time-limited or time-unlimited groups, unstructured process groups, or psychoeducationally structured groups. Time-unlimited groups have the advantage of facilitating dynamics through the development of transference and reenactment of family-of-origin interactional patterns. Over the course of time, the client is able to work through problematic patterns of behavior and to practice new, more adaptive ones. Time-unlimited groups may not be appropriate, however, for participants who are beginning group treatment and who are willing to make only a time-limited commitment to treatment. In addition, time-unlimited groups may foster dependency and delay goal-oriented work. Finally, time-unlimited groups may not meet the procedural needs of the organization.

The time-limited group, however, is more focused and deliberately structured for goal-oriented work, such as relief of symptoms, normalization of reactions to the experience (e.g., feeling "crazy," doubting own sense of reality, self-blame), sharing and reliving the trauma, resistance, grief work, and beginning to develop new, more adaptive behaviors. Such an approach discourages the progression of a sense of helplessness and dependency on authority figures and focuses on interactions with others within the context of themes associated with sexual abuse. Group dynamics and processes are not stressed; that is, personal defenses, dynamics, and patterns of interaction, although not ignored, are not processed in-depth; instead, members are referred for work in individual therapy. A fifteen-week time limit is appropriate, as it both allows time for presentation of didactic material and is of sufficient length to facilitate more in-depth processing of group dynamics.

A comprehensive review of the literature and an analysis of the needs of survivors of sexual abuse suggest that a time-limited, structured group program is most appropriate for this population. It may also best serve the needs of professionals first beginning to conduct groups with survivors because it provides a clearly delineated framework and guides the beginner through each session.

THE FIT

It is appropriate for the group leaders to define the policies and parameters of their particular group. An example of such a policy statement is as follows:

> Only survivors of childhood sexual abuse, twenty-one years of age or older, who are currently participating in individual psychotherapy and who are not actively suicidal, substance abusing, or psychotic will participate in this group therapy program. Ninety-minute sessions will be held weekly for a fifteen-week period.

FINE POINTS

Development of the program will proceed in three stages.

Stage I: Preparing the Foundation

The first stage of implementation begins once the decision has been made to conduct a group and the context has been assessed as appropriate. It is then necessary to define the specific policies of the program, based on the needs of the particular target population. A review of the literature on sexual abuse and incest will aid in the delineation of common themes and issues relevant to this population. While developing the didactic portion of each session, specific attention should be paid to the sequencing of themes and the particular needs of the population. Training issues for the therapist include didactic information about sexual abuse and incest, developing therapeutic skills in group dynamics, and processing personal reactions to the subject matter. Training and supervision for the beginning therapist should be ongoing throughout the program.

Finally, potential group members must be solicited and screened for suitability before the group is formed. Soliciting prospective clients should begin early enough to allow time for screening of all new members. This involves disseminating information about the group to all potential referral sources in advance of the projected start-up date. Successful networking is an invaluable resource for professionals interested in working with this population.

Other factors, such as time constraints of the sponsoring organization, should be considered when organizing the group. Individual psychotherapy services should be available for prospective clients in need of such services prior to participation. It is also important to take into account the existence of other groups in the geographic area that serve this population. Although this does not automatically discount the usefulness of the program, it may result in competition for group members.

If this group program is to be used for training purposes, the trainee role of the facilitator is another factor that may affect implementation of the program. Potential clients may be resistant to joining a group run by trainees. The training nature of the group must be discussed with each potential member prior to the first meeting. Training requirements may interfere with the implementation of the group. For example, clients may object to video and/or audiotaping of group sessions. This may be important for training purposes but may be unwarranted therapeutically. Careful screening of each member is critical, due to the wide range of behaviors often exhibited by this population.

Stage II: The Screening Intake

Each prospective participant meets individually with the cofacilitators for an in-depth interview to assess motivation, individual issues, interpersonal skills, and readiness for the group experience and general suitability for the group. A structured intake interview is used. Goals and structure of the group are discussed; fees are set. Clients are asked to complete a supplemental background questionnaire, depression inventory, and symptom checklist.

Stage III: Sum and Substance

The group is structured as a thematic, psychoeducational intervention. Ninety-minute sessions are held weekly for fifteen weeks. Each session follows the same basic format, with the psychoeducational theme varying from week to week (see Table 4.1). Sequencing of each theme is designed to enable the development of trust and to allow for improvement of symptomatic behaviors. Survivors

TABLE 4.1. Sample Weekly Schedule

The group will be meeting weekly, on Tuesday evenings, for 15 weeks, from 7:30 to 9:00 p.m. in Room 154.

1.	Introduction	9.	Unstructured session
2.	Trust/Safety	10.	Unstructured session
3.	Explorations of emotions and beliefs	11.	Unstructured session
4.	Disclosure	12.	Unstructured session
5.	Sexuality and intimacy	13.	Unstructured session
6.	Impact of abuse and coping	14.	Toward termination
7.	Family dynamics	15.	Termination
8.	Processing of memories		

are encouraged to disclose their experience to the group and to share the experience of the trauma. They are taught to deal with worsening of symptoms and to develop ways of coping that facilitate healing. The individual is then able to establish a new perspective on the incestuous experience, interpret and understand its personal meaning within the context of his/her adult life, and begin to develop future goals.

STRUCTURE

1. Sessions one through ten begin with a brief didactic presentation (five to ten minutes) by one or both of the group facilitators. This presentation is based upon the weekly theme. Specific activities vary each session, including, for example, experiential exercises, reading prose or poetry, disseminating information, or doing a creative activity. Sessions eleven to fifteen are less structured sessions, with content determined by the group members themselves. Sessions fourteen and fifteen address issues of termination.

2. Following the presentation, each group member is asked to "check in." The participant is asked what he/she has been doing/thinking/feeling about the previous week's session and if he/she would like some time during the current session to dis-

cuss something with the group. The check-in is a structured way of quickly assessing the state of each group member at the beginning of the group session. Each group member is addressed during this go-around, with lengthy discussion delayed for later in the session.*

3. After each member has checked in, the group begins the general discussion, as initiated by the group members.
4. Closure occurs with a final go-around to "check out" how each member is responding to the group's discussion and how he/she is feeling. This checking-out exercise helps reground the members in the present "real world," as they prepare to leave the evening's session (see Table 4.2).

The Personnel

Two group facilitators are required to lead this group. Different rationales have been offered for preferred gender and/or gender combination. (Refer to p. 25, "Group Organization and Structure," for a review of this issue.) The decision regarding facilitator gender should be made on the basis of the specific group to be run.

The Resources

Infrastructure and facilities: It is necessary to procure the use of a permanent facility prior to the onset of the program. Fee for rental of any facility should be discussed at this time. Rooms sufficiently large enough to comfortably accommodate eight to ten people, with proper ventilation and heating, will be required.

Materials: Video and/or audiotapes and a camcorder and/or tape recorder may be required for training purposes. References, handouts, and materials listed in session protocols are to be distributed during that particular session.

---

*Frequently, clients will respond with a noncommittal response, such as "I'm fine," at check-in/out time. People often say only what they need to, to get by. It is wise not to accept this response unconditionally, but instead, to explore if there is a way group members can tell the group that they are not fine, that they are unable to deal with what they are feeling/experiencing with the group at that time.

TABLE 4.2. General Structure for Weekly Meetings

1.	Didactic presentation by group facilitators
2.	Group members will be asked to "check in"
3.	Group discussion on the weekly theme presentation
4.	Summary of the session and the themes that have been raised
5.	Closure, "checking-out" time, with each member
6.	Relaxation exercises

Financial resources: A budget may need to be developed for this program, depending on where it will be conducted. It is suggested that this program be implemented within the organizational unit of a training clinic. All costs (photocopying, rent for use of rooms, audiovisual equipment) would then be absorbed by the general operating budget of the clinic. Personnel involved in facilitating the group may need to receive salaries. Opportunity costs for personnel could include reduction in the number of individual clients seen or inability to participate in other educative experiences because of limited time available. The direct supervisor of the facilitators may need to be reimbursed. No other direct costs will be incurred from the implementation of this program, with the exception of photocopying and the cost of materials. The budget for these expenses is approximately $50 for the fifteen-week period.

Nonmonetary Incentives

The facilitators will receive supervised training in group therapy and in the subject area of sexual abuse and incest from professional therapists who have experience working with survivors of sexual abuse. This added skill will greatly increase their area of expertise and their sense of competence and self-esteem as budding psychotherapists. The supervisor will improve his/her supervisory skills through supervising others. Contact with the trainees will also be beneficial for the supervisor as it keeps him/her involved, active, and up-to-date in an emerging field. The clinic or practice acquires an additional service to offer the community. The participants will gain greater control over their lives and increased awareness of the effect of their incestuous experience on their current functioning. They will acquire new skills to help them move toward healthier human functioning.

Monetary Incentives

The clinic or practice will receive payment from each participant to cover some, or all, of the group's operating costs.

IMPLEMENTATION

Implementation of the program as designed will be facilitated by the use of the "DURABLE" strategy recommended by Maher and Bennett (1984). "DURABLE" activities include program personnel in interrelated activities that reflect **d**iscussion of the program, an **u**nderstanding of related concepts, **r**einforcement of participation, **a**cquisition of necessary resources, **b**uilding a team approach, **l**earning new skills, and **e**valuation of attitudes, skills, and knowledge.

THE EVALUATION PLAN

It is necessary to systematically evaluate this program to ensure a successful outcome. This can be accomplished by the agency or individual conducting the program or, possibly, may be formally linked with university faculty or graduate students. The final step of the problem-solving approach is useful for program evaluation. This involves clarifying the evaluation problem, planning and organizing resources to obtain the needed evaluation information, obtaining that information, analyzing and communicating the evaluation results to the client, and assessing the usefulness of the evaluation. Two primary methods of evaluation can be employed: Goal Attainment Scaling (GAS) and Program Satisfaction Questionnaires. Examples of evaluation questionnaires are included in Appendixes B, C, and D. These questionnaires should be administered as designated, at the end of each session, at the end of the fifteen-week unit, and again after three months for follow-up. In this way, successful and unsuccessful components of the program can be identified and corrected, if necessary. Issues of specific interest to the group can also be noted and incorporated into the ongoing program.

PART II:
SESSION PROTOCOLS

Self-knowledge and self-acceptance develop largely by inter-acting with others in a positive way.

J. Baker Miller

I DENY first and allow You to help me deny.
Then you deny—and I die!
I cannot allow that, the strengths in me shout out to be heard
But the roar of the pain splashes over us all
The wall goes on forever . . . but the corner reaches the end
Fighting to keep out of that corner is
fighting to keep out of that box.

To fight, to live, to breathe, to say
This is MY RIGHT TO BE HEARD.
It is also my right to decide when I no longer can
continue to fight.
When all the battles I can fight have been fought
and I decide to surrender
Know I have the strength!

The world has room for better fighters!
I will return in another life and use that knowledge you have shared with me
The outcome cannot be known before the beginning—there are no endings.
A circle of hope, even in despair.
A crown of jewels among the thorns.
We are all fragments—pieces of joy, pieces of pain.
To be sifted and molded—breaking apart to become each of us one,
Each of us all.

A. B., 1995, survivor of sexual abuse

Chapter 5

The Screening Intake

RATIONALE

Group therapy may not be advisable for all incest survivors. An assessment of the client's history, strengths and weaknesses, current life functioning, therapeutic issues and goals, and interpersonal and coping skills is necessary to determine the suitability of the group format for the particular client. The intake interview also allows clients an opportunity to meet the group facilitators, to determine if they would like to participate in the group, and if so, to become familiar with the group setting, design, and goals. Anxieties and concerns about participating in a group can be addressed at this time.

GOALS AND OBJECTIVES

1. Assess suitability of client for group participation.
2. Assess suitability of group in meeting client's therapeutic needs.
3. Allow client to meet group facilitators prior to first session.
4. Address client's questions, fears, and anxieties about partici-pation in the group.
5. Determine client's readiness and capacity for affect regulation.

MATERIALS

Intake questionnaire, paper and pen, and release forms.

PROCEDURE

Allot two hours for interview.

Welcome potential client and explain purpose of screening inter-view (to become better acquainted with client's history, issues, and therapeutic needs to determine if the group is appropriate).

Intake Questions

1. Demographic information: What is your name, address, telephone number, age, occupation, marital status, and number of children, if any.
2. Previous experience in therapy: Have you ever been in therapy before? Are you currently involved in individual therapy? (Obtain name of therapist now and address and release form at end of session.)
3. Motivation for therapy: Why would you like to participate in a group therapy program at this time?
4. Current life situation: What is going on in your life at the present time? (Ask about family, friends, school, work, leisure activities, health, financial status, and support systems.)
5. Childhood experiences: What was your childhood like? What was it like to grow up in your family? What were your mother/father/siblings like?
6. Incest history: Tell us what you can about your incest experience—Who was the perpetrator? How old were you when it began/ended? What happened? Was force used? What were you told at the time? What did you understand about what happened? How do you think it affected you? Did you ever try to tell anyone? What was their reaction? (Assess the client's ability to disclose, tolerate, and regulate anxiety and other emotions that may arise.)
7. Rule out *active** substance abuse: What is your medical history? What medications do you take? (These questions help differentiate between active and recreational abuse; in any event, it should be made clear that participants are expected to remain sober during the group sessions.)
8. Rule out *active* suicide ideation and intent: Did you ever feel so bad that you wanted to hurt yourself?

---

*The key criterion is *active* substance abuse, suicidal ideation, and/or psychosis. Do any of these issues interfere with the client's ability to benefit from group treatment? Would this behavior negatively affect other group members? "The ultimate question the therapist must ask is: Does this client have sufficient inner resources and few enough interfering factors that s/he could attend the group without becoming a casualty of the treatment process" (Briere, 1989, p. 144).

9. Rule out *active* psychosis.
10. Assess client's reaction to present interview: How do you feel now? How was it to talk about the incest with us? How do you think it will be to discuss it in a group?
11. Willingness to discuss abuse, expectations, and goals: Assess client's willingness to discuss some of the aspects of the abuse within the group setting. Discuss the client's expectations for therapy and set preliminary goals: What would you like to see occur in the group? What would you like to discuss? Are there any particular topics?
12. Explain group structure, content, and process to client: Do you have any questions about the group?

Relaxation Training Techniques

If the client is considered appropriate for participation in the group, teach him/her relaxation training techniques. Hand out written copy so the client can practice at home.

1. Introduce conceptual aspects of relaxation: "Frequently, when under stress, our bodies will show physical signs of tenseness. This tenseness can further exacerbate stress. Relaxation and a reduction of the bodily tension can reduce the effects of stress. It can reduce anxiety and allow you to regain control over a situation. Relaxation can be achieved through different means, such as tensing and releasing muscles, meditation, exercise, and a favorite activity. It is as much a state of mind as a physical state."
2. Ask client what it means to be relaxed: How will you give yourself permission to relax? What concerns do you have about this technique?
3. Present this technique as an active coping strategy that requires practice. Discuss with client why, when, and how he/she will practice. Anticipate problems that may occur. For example, the client may experience difficulty relaxing if techniques are first practiced in an agitated state. Also, rapid breathing may cause hyperventilation. This can be corrected by slowing down breathing and/or breathing into cupped

hands. Clients should be encouraged to use the technique(s) with which they are most comfortable.
4. Teach relaxation technique (Meichenbaum, 1985): "The relaxation coping skill involves your mastery and control in stressful situations. You will learn to control your breathing, to distract yourself from the stressful situation, and to progressively relax the major muscle groups in your body."

Breathing

"First, sit back comfortably, with your legs and back supported; relax your body; drop your shoulders; relax your hands; close your eyes. Expand your chest, breathing in deeply as you say *in* silently. Concentrate on your breathing. Breathe slowly. Next, hold your breath for about five seconds. Finally, exhale slowly and fully while saying *relax* and *calm* silently to yourself, relaxing your whole body. Repeat this second sequence for two minutes or until you feel your body relax and your heart rate slow down."

Demonstrate the technique for the client. Debrief the client: "How did this feel? Any difficulty with it? Did your mind wander? Did you experience any mental intrusions? What was intruding?"

Guided Imagery

"Try to stay relaxed. I would like you to create a picture in your mind's eye that would be very relaxing for you. What kind of picture would you create? Your picture could include stillness, warmth, calm feelings—lying on a beach in the hot sun or under a tree with the calm wind blowing—whatever relaxes you. Gently close your eyes. Picture an image. Raise your forefinger when you have it in your mind. Put your finger down when you lose the image. How long can you hold it?" Debrief the client using the questions under "Breathing."

Muscle Relaxation

"Lie back comfortably with your body supported so there is no need to tense your muscles. Relax." (Pause for two to three seconds.) "Concentrate on the feeling in your right hand. Tense that hand and then slowly relax the muscles." (Pause.) "Slowly tense and relax your right arm muscles." (Proceed with the tensing and relaxing exercise, covering the body's major muscle groups, pausing frequently, and urging client to let go and relax more and more after each stage of the exercise.). Debrief the client.

End of Intake Session

Following the relaxation training techniques:

1. Have client review efforts and make self-improvements.
2. Obtain release signatures.
3. Confirm date, time, and location of first group session.

Chapter 6

The Group Sessions

SESSION 1:
STARTING OUT—THE INTRODUCTION

Rationale

To facilitate successful group treatment, it is necessary to first establish guidelines for group formation and the development of group norms. The development of group cohesion and a safe, supportive setting, which is conducive to open discussion, acceptance, and approval, is critical if the therapeutic objectives are to be achieved.

Goals and Objectives

1. Acknowledge common reasons for participating in the group.
2. Introduce group members and facilitator(s).
3. Discuss organization of group, structure, themes, and process.
4. Establish ground rules.
5. Establish goals for each member within group.
6. Discuss fears about, and expectations for, group.
7. Identify strategies for taking care of oneself.
8. Review relaxation techniques.

Materials

Poster board and markers; weekly evaluation questionnaires.

Procedure

Check-In and Introduction to Group

Acknowledge Common Reason for Participating in the Group

A close family member or friend has sexually molested all group members. Immediately begin "breaking the silence" surrounding sexual abuse; establish norms for discussion of the topic.

> Welcome to the group. We are all here for a common purpose—to begin breaking the silence surrounding sexual abuse. A close family member or friend has sexually molested each of you. Each of you may have varying degrees of memory about having been sexually abused, and you may have kept it a secret for many years. We hope that this group will help you begin talking about your experience and about how it has affected you thus far. Disclosing what you can about your experience to this group, to the extent that you judge safe, reduces the secrecy surrounding it and promotes healing.
>
> We do not expect the process of healing to be finished at the end of the fifteen weeks. This group is a beginning step toward understanding and integrating your experience of incest. We hope you will learn new strategies for coping with the effects of that experience, alter some behaviors, thoughts, and cognitions which may no longer be helpful, and develop some behaviors which will serve you more effectively and adaptively today. At the end of the fifteen weeks, we hope that each of you will evaluate where you have been and where you would like to go. At that point, we can plan the next step in the process that will be most beneficial for you.

Introduce Group Members and Facilitators

Introductions should begin with the facilitators and continue around the group, allowing each member to introduce himself/herself.

> As we begin, let's go around and introduce ourselves to one another. Please say your name, why you have decided to join

the group, and anything else about your current life situation (marriage, children, employment, etc.) that you would like to share with the members. . . . My name is . . . (facilitator will briefly share something with the group).

Discuss Organization of Group, Structure, Themes, and Process

The group is a time-limited, structured, psychoeducational program specifically designed to treat survivors of sexual abuse. The group will continue for fifteen weeks, ninety minutes per week. It is structured around specific themes that have been found to most affect survivors of sexual abuse. In the past, the themes have included trust, anger and emotions, coping strategies, sexuality, disclosure, shame, blame and responsibility, confrontation, family dynamics, etc. We would like to develop the agenda based on the specific needs of this particular group, so we invite your input. The group is psychoeducational in that we will offer didactic information about different aspects of sexual abuse. We will begin each group by checking in with you to see how you are feeling and how the group has affected you over the past week. We will then present the theme of the current week, either by providing didactic information or through an exercise. After the group discussion, we will then check out with each member, again, to see how you are feeling and how you have responded to what has transpired in the group.

Establish Ground Rules

Ground rules should be acceptable to all members of the group, with some exceptions. No flexibility exists with rules about confidentiality and its limits or about the substance-free nature of the group.

One of our primary goals for this group is to establish a safe place in which you can explore the impact of the past abuse. To that end, we would like to establish some basic ground rules for the group. Again, we invite you to participate in establishing these rules.

Confidentiality: "The first rule we would like to discuss is that of confidentiality. Anything that is discussed here will remain within the group and will not be discussed outside the group, with two exceptions. If we believe the danger exists that a group member will hurt himself/herself or someone else, we are obligated to consult with outside sources. We also reserve the right to maintain open communication with your individual therapists to provide continuity of services to you."

Certain issues surrounding confidentiality should be open to group discussion. These might include rules regarding conversations among group members outside the group, the possibility of meeting a group member in a public place—whether to or how to acknowledge them—and exchange of phone numbers.

Depending on the circumstances, it may be necessary to extend the limits of confidentiality to include supervision. It also may be necessary to request permission from the group to audio- and/or videotape the sessions for training purposes. In this case, all members must agree unanimously, with the understanding that they will always know when they are being taped and that the tape can be turned off at any time.

Substance-Free Group: "No member of the group will come to the group while under the influence of drugs or alcohol."

Safety: "There will be no abuse of any kind in the group (physical, emotional, sexual). Also, no unsolicited physical contact will be allowed. We ask that you try not to leave the group during the ninety-minute session. This is for your own safety and also because it is disruptive to the group process. If it ever seems necessary to leave, please do not exit the building without first checking back with us. We all will be concerned for your safety and well-being."

Pass Option: "Each member of this group must progress at his/her own rate. No one will be pushed to participate or disclose more than he/she is able to at any given point. Each member can choose the 'pass option' at any time."

The one exception to this might be on the evening of formal disclosure of the abuse. At this time, the group member will be asked to relate some part of his/her story, to break the silence. The ability to begin talking about the abuse must be a primary criterion for participating in the group.

Commitment: Suggest adopting a ground rule about commitment to participation in the full fifteen weeks. Discuss the importance of commitment to the process of healing, as well as to the overall group process. Group sessions may be very difficult at times, and the member may prefer to avoid them. The member should then make an extra effort to attend and discuss his/her reluctance. If, however, the group member decides not to continue with the group, request that he/she come in for one last session to discuss the reasons for his/her decision. Discuss therapeutic benefit of this parting session to group and to individual.

Ask group members to suggest any ground rules they would like to include. *List ground rules on a piece of poster board so that they are clearly visible throughout each session.*

Establish Goals for Each Member Within the Group

"What would each of you like to accomplish during the next fifteen weeks?" Go around to each group member and record goals, to be reviewed at the end of fifteen weeks. Make goals as specific and measurable as possible (e.g., "How will you [we] know you have increased your self-esteem?"). Remember that it may be enough of a goal just to attend each session.

Discuss Fears About, and Expectations for, Group

"Beginning a group therapy program can be an intimidating endeavor. What are some of the fears and concerns you might have about the group? What can be done to reduce those fears? What are some of your expectations for the group?" Allow each member the opportunity to respond.

Identify Strategies for Taking Care of Oneself

We hope that you will find the next fifteen weeks helpful to you in dealing with the effects of sexual abuse. The process may also be stressful and emotionally exhausting at times, demanding the investment of a great deal of energy. It may not be the best time to begin anything new or to make major changes that would cause additional stress.

We would like you to begin thinking about what you do to take care of yourself during stressful times. In the past, you may have developed some coping strategies that were adaptive in an abnormal situation. These strategies may no longer be effective in reducing the stress and anxiety. Throughout the group, we hope to provide alternatives to replace these noneffective methods.

Open group to discussion: "What coping mechanisms have you developed to help you deal with stress in the past? Are they still effective and adaptive? What have you found to be helpful?" Different ways to take care of oneself may include physical as well as emotional care: exercise, healthy diet, developing support systems, utilizing individual therapy to process group issues, relaxation techniques, warm baths, etc.

Reintroduce Relaxation Technique

Refer to the detailed discussion in the section "Relaxation Training Techniques" (Meichenbaum, 1985), in Chapter 5.

Solicit Group Input

Ask members about themes they would like to discuss in the upcoming weeks.

Summarize Discussion

Give a brief summary of the first week's session.

Check-Out with Each Member

Ask members how they are feeling and elicit any thoughts they might have about the group at this point.

SESSION 2:
TRUST AND SAFETY

Rationale

Trust is an especially sensitive issue for survivors of incest because of their betrayal by a trusted individual. Trust among group members can facilitate achievement of their goals. Explicit discussion of the issue of trust allows recognition of the impact of the early betrayal, provides an understanding of current difficulties in interpersonal relationships, and highlights the group members' commonality of experience in this area. Group members are encouraged to deal effectively with their feelings and experiences within the context of a safe, accepting relationship. In the group, the members gain a sense of one another; they begin to develop a relationship. This session is a preliminary step toward the upcoming disclosure. The context of the relationship within which the secret is disclosed is critical. Disclosure does not necessarily create connection, but connection allows disclosure. When a safe relationship is established, the person with whom you have begun to connect can know about your experiences and still be accepting. The context of the relationship creates the healing of disclosure. Shame, secrecy, and stigma are reduced within a safe, accepting relationship and a sharing of common experiences.

Different aspects of the group process, or of the techniques used within the group, may paradoxically decrease the group's sense of safety. It is important to address these issues at some point, processing the feelings generated by particular situations. One example of this is prolonged silence. Silence sometimes serves to increase the level of anxiety or other emotions within the group. This may replicate particular family dynamics; some survivors have reported that such an atmosphere feels punishing to them. It is important to acknowledge the silence and the different emotions it may engender. For example, it may suffice to recognize the discomfort: "I have noticed different reactions when the silence is prolonged. Sometimes people feel anxious or uncomfortable with silence. What is it like for you?"

Various techniques may unwittingly evoke different visceral reactions from the group. More stressful internal experience and increased anxiety may result more from a guided imagery exercise than from a sentence completion inventory that allows a more intellectualized response. It is important to be aware of the sometimes subtle influence of different interventions.

Goals and Objectives

1. Define qualities essential to trust, and facilitate development of trust within the group by highlighting commonalities of experience in this area.
2. Understand how sexual abuse has affected their ability to trust in self and in others.
3. Develop an atmosphere that encourages disclosure.
4. Explore therapeutic rationales for discussion of incest-related topics.

Materials

Drawing paper and crayons; weekly evaluation questionnaires.

Procedure

Check-In

Begin the evening's session by checking in with each group member to determine his/her reactions to the previous session and how the group has affected him/her during the past week.

Introduce the Evening's Theme—Trust/Safety

Children instinctively trust those who care for them. Their trust develops as their needs are met consistently and dependably. When children are sexually abused, their needs are not considered, but become secondary to the needs of another. Sexual abuse shatters trust and teaches children that it is not safe to respond to their basic instincts.

Guided Imagery Exercise

Explain purpose of guided imagery exercise and give overview. Guided imagery has been used to introduce relaxation and soothing imagery. In addition, it can be a nonthreatening way of enabling the client to create a safe place in his/her mind, in which he/she can then more easily explore traumatic memories. This approach can be helpful in promoting a sense of independence and self-power (see McCann and Pearlman, 1990).

> Please sit back and close your eyes if you feel comfortable doing so. We would like you to imagine what trust means to you. . . . Think about what it means to trust. . . . Whom did you trust as a child? . . . What special qualities did that person have that led you to trust? . . . How has your trust been violated? . . . Whom do you trust in your life now? . . . What does that trust look like? . . . What color does it take? . . . What form? . . . What texture? . . . What qualities in you are brought out when you trust someone? . . . Are you trustworthy? . . . How do you know you can trust someone? . . . What does that trust look like? . . . What color does it take? . . . What form? . . . What texture? . . . Imagine what trust would look like/feel like, if you could draw it. . . .

Have members open their eyes and ask them to *draw what trust means to them*. Have each member discuss his/her drawings, if he/she feels comfortable doing so. Point out commonalities and similar responses. List the range of reactions; emphasize the benefits of trusting when sufficient safety is ascertained. Discuss specifically how people think/feel about trust. Discuss how distrust affects people and can be an obstacle to establishing/maintaining relationships. How did abuse affect their ability to trust? How does that ability differ today?

Discuss Different Types of Trust

Trust In Others: Why is trust essential to establishing/maintaining relationships? How was trust betrayed by the perpetrator or by others who did not stop the abuse or believe it happened? (Use questions asked during the guided imagery to focus discussion.)

Trust In Self: "You need to learn to trust yourself; listen to what your body tells you, and have faith in your intuition/perceptions."

Many adult survivors have difficulty believing their perceptions, senses, and feelings. They do not trust their instincts and continually doubt themselves. Survivors often believe they must be crazy—they have been told that so often, or their reality has been twisted.

Discuss Obstacles to Trusting Self

Dissociation: Explore the following questions with group members:

> To trust your thoughts and perceptions, you need to be present, to pay attention to what is going on inside you. What happens when you begin to dissociate? Does this happen in other places? What is that like for you? What was an effective coping skill when growing up may no longer be the appropriate skill for healing. How can you learn to be present, to pay attention to your thoughts and feelings? What do you do/think/feel when you begin to space out? How can you intervene?

Negative Messages: Verbal abuse resulted in dysfunctional cognitions today. Survivors need to learn to pay attention to their intuitions and dispute their faulty cognitions.

Setting limits is one way to overcome obstacles to trusting in oneself. "Saying 'no' establishes boundaries, helps you to protect yourself, and gives you control over the choices and decisions in your life."

Introduce the Topic of Safety

Stress commitment to safety of group. The goal is to create an atmosphere that encourages open discussion of the issues which concern each member and to minimize the risk of revictimization. How is this achieved? Certain measures are taken to maximize feelings about safety: ground rules, check-ins, discussions of fears, expectations, goals, etc. *Safety* is the primary overriding factor for the group. To that end, it is necessary to discuss the rationales for talking about the different incest-related topics.

Allow group members to discuss why they think it would help them to talk about their experiences (break the silence), how they have coped in the past, and how they have trusted in the past and the present. Questions to consider include: What drives people to need to tell? What would it be like if they did not discuss the actual details of the incest? How does telling help heal? What is it about the group that facilitates healing?

Summarize Discussion

Practice Relaxation Technique

Check-out with Each Group Member

Assess emotional state. Gauge reactions to the evening's discussion.

Case Example

Meredith is a thirty-year-old, single white female and mother of two young children. She first sought therapy during a period of marital conflict, which ultimately ended in divorce. She moved into her parents' home after the divorce and has remained there to raise her children as a stay-at-home mom.

Meredith was first sexually abused at the age of six by a neighborhood baby-sitter, then again at the age of twelve by a family friend. In high school and later in college, she was also forcibly raped. For each instance, Meredith described a sense of confusion and powerlessness to resist. She gradually began to internalize feelings of shame, self-blame, and responsibility, as she was uncertain about her own role in these events. Meredith described her passive acceptance of boundary violations over the years and her inability to set limits, safeguard her physical integrity, or take control of her person. She blindly trusted that people would do the right thing in this world and struggled with evidence against this.

When Meredith was thirteen, her world was thrown into turmoil when her parents separated. The separation disrupted Meredith's already fragile sense of self and feelings of safety. She became anorexic and was unable to fully break this cycle until her parents reunited a year and a half later.

Meredith married the first man who was nice to her. The marriage began to deteriorate after the birth of their first child. Her husband worked long hours and devoted much time to many personal hobbies and interests. He became verbally abusive and demeaning and ceased considering Meredith's needs in his decision making. She began to feel invisible. The fear that her daughter would grow up in that kind of household provided the only motivation for her to leave the marriage.

Themes of shame, guilt, blame, and responsibility pervaded Meredith's participation in the group. She quickly assumed the role of caretaker and maintained careful monitoring of the other participants' moods. She was able to feel outrage when confronted with her fellow group members' stories of abuse and defend their rights for personal control. She provided much-needed support and nurturance as they recounted their experiences but was unable to apply those emotions to her own self. For example, Meredith would frequently justify a new boyfriend's emotionally abusive and severely restricting behavior toward her as proof that he loved her, but she could not see the lack of trust or respect inherent in such behavior. Instead, she would question what more she could do to make everything all right again. Accepting blame, she would become apologetic and contrite when faced with his ire, whether deserved or not.

When angry emotions surfaced in the group, Meredith initially would assume responsibility for soothing the group, often placating others at her own expense, or she would shut down emotionally as she became overwhelmed with anxiety. The group began to challenge her to identify her rights and responsibilities in a more rational manner and to set limits with regard to what behaviors she would or would not accept from others in her life. Meredith slowly began to define clear limits and boundaries that allowed her to maintain a distinct sense of self, while still caring for others. She began to assert herself and to take more control as she sought to have her own needs met.

SESSION 3:
EXPLORATION OF EMOTIONS AND BELIEFS

Rationale

"The group is a unique context and catalyst for breaking through denial and allowing the exploration and ventilation of feelings and beliefs" (Courtois, 1988, p. 248). As such, it serves as an ideal forum for the examination, experience, and resolution of sometimes conflicting, confusing, and ambivalent emotions of anger, rage, grief, sadness, fear, hatred, and love. In addition, identifying and challenging distorted messages and beliefs and maladaptive behavior patterns from childhood are facilitated within the supportive group framework. This session begins a process that encourages the verbal expression of feelings and helps prepare the client to deal with unpleasant and threatening emotions associated with the abuse.

Goals and Objectives

1. Increase awareness and identification of feelings.
2. Identify different emotions that may be associated with the sexual abuse (including anger, betrayal, sadness, vulnerability, pleasure, fear, guilt, and shame).
3. Facilitate expression of different emotions.
4. Encourage members to be responsive and supportive to other group members.

Materials

Identifying Feelings handout (see pp. 79-80) and pencils; weekly evaluation questionnaires.

Procedure

Check-In

Begin the evening's session by checking in with each group member to determine his/her reactions to the previous session and how the group has affected him/her during the past week.

Introduce the Evening's Theme—Feelings

Discuss the myriad of emotions that they may have felt before, during, and after the incest. If preferred, specific discussion about anger may be substituted for this session (see "Alternative Theme").

Distribute Handout and Pencil to Each Group Member

Allow ten minutes to complete. Discuss responses. What is the primary emotion they experience (e.g., anger, sadness, or guilt)? What fears do they have about expressing other feelings (e.g., will be overwhelmed by anger or drown in sadness; touch on feelings of vulnerability, helplessness, powerlessness, and strength)? What is the worst that could happen? What are the chances of that happening? How would they cope with it if it did happen?

Summarize Discussion

Highlight each member's positive and negative ways of coping with affect.

Prepare Group for Disclosure in Next Session

Integrate ideas of safety, trust, and the context of the relationship as precursors to the healing aspects of disclosure. Discuss this as a process that will continue throughout the group. Discuss members' previous experience with disclosing and reactions to it. Members are encouraged to say something about their experiences to gain feedback from the group, but each client must control his/her disclosure. Disclosure can be structured in a manner that feels safe/tolerable/comfortable to each member (e.g., being asked questions, free-flowing disclosure, writing out a story and reading it to the group). Ask members whether they prefer time-limited or open-ended disclosure. Questions may be written out on poster board to serve as guidelines for disclosure. Members are encouraged to think about the different options for the next session.

Practice Relaxation Technique

Check-Out with Each Group Member

Assess emotional state; gauge reactions to the evening's discussion.

Alternative Theme—Anger

1. Discuss functions of anger. It can be destructive, and it can mask other feelings such as sadness, pain, and loss. It can be used as a defense against vulnerability, and it can be used constructively to get needs met. Questions useful for exploring this emotion include the following:

   • How have you used anger in the past?
   • How has it been used against you?
   • How would you like to use anger in your life?
   • What do you get angry about?
   • How do you express your anger? Externally? Internally?
   • How can your anger be used constructively?
   • What may anger mask?
   • Is there a risk involved in uncovering what is behind the anger?
   • What would happen if the anger was taken away?
   • What would it be like/feel like/mean to you if you felt [another emotion] mixed in with the anger?

2. Explore whether one person's feelings generalize to the whole group. Has anyone else ever felt this way? "Who in the group do you think might feel the same or understand you best?"
3. Encourage the group members to be as concrete as possible in their discussion. Monitor group members' emotional state. Check in frequently: "This can be frightening. How are you doing? How many people are feeling nervous? anxious? nauseous?" Does anyone seem to be dissociating?

Rage and anger are emotions that frequently emerge after an abusive and exploitative experience. The anger may be expressed in a variety of ways, as a reaction to the "wrongness" of the abuse, against the lack of protection by the nonoffending parent, or directed toward the perpetrator. At times the anger may be turned inward as self-hatred. The hostility may be expressed inappropriately at times in different interpersonal interactions. Within the therapy setting, transferential reactions may trigger the survivor's anger. For example, the similarity of the therapist to the former abuser or feelings of abandonment, rejection, or lack of protection may elicit a strong rage reaction. Such reactions may result from benign, caring interactions, as well as from clearly inappropriate responses on the part of the therapist (Briere, 1989).

Case Example

Tammy is a thirty-year-old, married, well-educated female who has been employed by an insurance company for eight years. Her father had abused her until his death when she was ten, but she only began to remember details of the abuse during the past year. Tammy had a history of frequent mood swings and uncontrolled anger, especially when feeling vulnerable or used. Conflict and explosive anger had repeatedly interfered with her personal and professional relationships. Early treatment focused on her anger in relationships and afforded some relief.

After a four-year period of "calm," during which she married and moved away from her family, the anger returned with a vengeance, accompanied by nightmares and depression. She returned to individual psychotherapy and, for the first time, began talking about her abusive experience. Treatment then focused on a delayed, complicated grieving of her father's death and an exploration of the memories of sexual abuse.

Her father's death had never been discussed within the family, and active mourning was discouraged. Feelings of grief, guilt, and relief intermingled as Tammy attempted to understand her complicated relationship with her abuser. She reported being his favorite, but her close relationship with him was later disrupted by his illness. On the other hand, Tammy was constantly afraid of her father, who physically and emotionally abused her in addition to the sexual abuse. She remembered being terrified of being left alone with him, yet at times she felt she replaced her mother in his affections. She remembered his anger toward her when she would wipe his kisses away or when she would hang a DO NOT DISTURB sign on her bedroom door.

A large part of Tammy's anger was also directed toward her mother, who not only did not protect her from her father, but also emotionally abused her and expected her to become the second parent after his death. As the eldest child, Tammy assumed the leadership role, helping to keep the family afloat. This anger and resentment began to seep out as Tammy became an adult, often uncontrollable and at inappropriate times.

Tammy sought group therapy as an adjunct to her individual treatment, hoping to find support from others who shared a similar experience. She feared that she might have fabricated the abuse and doubted the veracity of her memories. Group participation was another way for her to validate her memories, test her reality, and move past her denial of the abuse.

During her participation in the group program, her need to be in a position of control and leadership coexisted with a need to be supported, protected, and understood within the group. Tammy alternated between virulent outbursts expressing her dissatisfaction and disagreement with the process and structure of the group and silent, isolationist, nonparticipation in the group discussions. She frequently complained about the inherent structure and pace of the psychoeducational group format and deemed it unprofessional and unsupportive. The need to dictate the group process seemed to be an effort to control the anxiety stirred up by group discussions, yet in many respects, this threatened the other members and undermined the sense of safety within the group.

Efforts were made to address this anger within the group, both from Tammy's viewpoint and from that of the other members. Reactions were reflected back to the participants, and connections were made to past experiences. The meaning of the anger was explored and analyzed from three perspectives: the general meaning of anger, each individual's expression/understanding of his/her anger based upon personal experiences, and the meaning of the anger as expressed within the group.

Members were unable to fully articulate their own experiences with anger because they were reacting to Tammy (identifying her as an abuser threatening their safety) and the group facilitators (fearing they would not be protected from further abuse). Tammy did realize that the role she sought in the group paralleled the one she had held in her family, as protector and defender of the others. This may have stirred up the feelings of helplessness, lack of protection, and vulnerability that she had experienced as a child, resulting in an expression of her anger and resentment. Tammy was unable to accept support, understanding, or nurturance from the group facilitators ("parents"), and she rejected their attempts to reflect this back to her. She was, however, able to absorb the support and understanding of the other participants, who validated her reality and helped decrease the denial with which she struggled.

Identifying Feelings

1. When I was a child I felt . . . . when . . . .

Happy _____

Sad _____

Scared _____

Angry _____

Excited _____

Disappointed _____

Lonely _____

Worried _____

Ashamed _____

Special _____

Guilty _____

2. I usually felt . . . .

_____

_____

_____

_____

_____

3. When I felt . . . . I would . . . .

Happy _____

Sad _____

Scared _____

Angry _____

Excited _____

Disappointed _____

Lonely _____

Worried _____

Ashamed _____

Special _____

Guilty _____

4. Today I feel . . . . when . . . .

Happy _____

Sad _____

Scared _____

Angry _____

Excited _____

Disappointed _____

Lonely _____

Worried _____

Ashamed _____

Special _____

Guilty _____

5. I generally feel . . . .

_____

_____

_____

_____

_____

_____

6. When I feel . . . .

Happy _____

Sad _____

Scared _____

Angry _____

Excited _____

Disappointed _____

Lonely _____

Worried _____

Ashamed _____

Special _____

Guilty _____

SESSION 4:
BREAKING THE SILENCE—DISCLOSURE

Rationale

Telling one's story, breaking the secrecy surrounding childhood sexual abuse, within the context of a safe, supportive environment has been called a "ritual of mastery leading to psychological growth" (Gold-Steinberg and Buttenheim, 1993, p. 173). It offers the survivor the opportunity to examine erroneous constructions of the incest experience and to reframe them in terms of adult understanding. The context of the relationship within which the secret is disclosed is critical. Shame and secrecy are reduced by an accepting relationship and shared experiences. Sharing and reliving the trauma with those who have had similar experiences also helps reduce the stigma and isolation frequently associated with the abuse. Disclosure can lead to the beginning of new conceptualizations of self and others and alternative actions for change and growth.

As preparation for the disclosure, it is helpful to first assess the individual's previous experiences with telling. How was their telling received? How did they feel after telling? Also, allow the survivors time to reflect on their hopes, expectations, and fears about the current disclosure. This can be done during the intake session, at the end of the previous session, or at the beginning of this session.

Goals and Objectives

1. Publicly acknowledge, name, and conceptualize the experience of sexual abuse within the context of a supportive group relationship.
2. Promote resolution of isolation and shame.
3. Work through incest trauma and trauma of disclosure.
4. Correct erroneous constructions of incest experience.
5. Provide a corrective interpersonal experience.

Materials

Poster board with questions to guide disclosure; weekly evaluation questionnaires.

Procedure

Check-In

Discuss Why Disclosure Is Healing

Abuse is no longer a secret, and reality is acknowledged; shame and stigma are reduced; understanding and support are received; etc. Explore expectations, fears, and hopes for this disclosure.

Provide Structure and Ground Rules for Disclosure

1. Establish time limit per person, unlimited or restricted.
2. Members should specify if they want to be asked questions, interrupted while telling their story, or responded to after they relate their experience. What would be the best method for them?
3. Remind members that they can stop any time prior to end of time limit; at minimum, they should try to say their age at time of abuse and name the perpetrator. If someone is unable to recount his/her experience, process what makes it difficult to disclose (fears, what he/she imagines will happen if the story is told).

Encourage Each Member to "Tell His/Her Story"

Questions to guide disclosure:

- How old were you?
- Who was/were the perpetrator(s)?
- Where did it happen?
- How long did it go on? How frequent?
- Did you tell anyone? How did they react?
- What did you do to cope at the time?
- When/why did the abuse stop?
- Whom have you told since the abuse ended?
- How did their response affect you?
- In what ways do you cope with the abuse today?

Relaxation Exercise

Check-Out—Debrief

Allow survivors to reflect on the telling after it has occurred. What was it like to tell? How does this recounting compare to other times? What was it like to listen to others? What sense can they make of the abuse now? Predict reactions that may occur after the members leave the evening's group. What are some ways they can take care of themselves?

Case Example

Abbe is a forty-nine-year-old female living on disability and diagnosed as manic-depressive. She relates her experiences of telling her story:

> When I first told my parents of the incest with my brother, it was while on my first psych ward over twenty years ago. I don't remember my father's reaction. . . . I will never forget my mother's: "Oh, is that all? Well now there is no problem. We thought you were having an affair with your girlfriend . . . "
>
> I am an incest survivor abused by my older brother. He was thirteen and I was eleven when the abuse occurred. . . . For him, it was a time of sexual awakening; for me, still in the middle of my childhood, it was a time of loss. His physical experimentation upon me was the beginning of the death of our relationship. . . . A physical death could not have been worse, yet it took me sixteen years to realize and accept that a death had occurred.
>
> Twenty-two years ago this past December, I was in the throes of a suicidal depression. Most of the doctors who treated me did not want me working on the incest because they felt it would set my manic-depression off. . . . I felt exactly as if this was something I should be able to deal with myself. . . .
>
> The incest had occurred sixteen years before and I had told no one, mainly because I thought my father would kill my brother. . . . It was only later that I realized there had been a death anyway, and I had never had a chance to mourn my brother's passing.

SESSION 5:
THE AFTERMATH OF THE ABUSE

Rationale

Childhood sexual abuse results in both short- and long-term effects in many domains of human functioning. Survivors frequently deny and/or minimize the effects of the abuse because of the shame and stigma that are associated with it. Untreated effects may become chronic and may influence the individual's continuing development and mental health. The consequences of childhood sexual abuse, the effects of the trauma, and the connection with resulting mental health disturbances need to be explicated, acknowledged, and understood therapeutically.

It is often helpful at this time to discuss past coping strategies to understand how they helped in the past and to evaluate their current usefulness. It is also important for each group member to begin to develop new coping skills to replace those that are no longer effective. A list of common defenses used to help the individual survive with the abuse is included later in this session.

A person can use many different strategies to facilitate the healing process. One may choose to express the affective and cognitive aspects of the experience through writing, artwork, or drama. Another avenue of expression may be political advocacy, through such organizations as VOICES (Victims of Incest Can Emerge Survivors), Mothers Alliance for Rights of Children, or the National Coalition Against Sexual Assault. States may have governmental organizations that develop policies directed toward combating child abuse of all types. An example of this is New Jersey's Governor's Task Force on Child Abuse.

Goals and Objectives

1. Identify and understand the effects of past sexual abuse on each individual's development and his/her current cognitive, emotional, social, sexual, spiritual, and physical functioning.
2. Begin the process of mourning losses resulting from the abuse.
3. Understand how they coped with the abuse.
4. Develop new skills to facilitate healing.

Materials

Impact of Childhood Sexual Abuse Questionnaire (see pp. 86-88) and the Defenses handout (see p. 89); weekly evaluation questionnaires.

Procedure

Check-In

Have Group Members Complete Questionnaire

Questions for Discussion

Raise questions for each member to answer:

- How has the abuse affected their lives? Discuss in terms of physical, emotional, spiritual, sexual, and cognitive effects.
- How did they learn to deal with the abuse while it was occurring?
- How would their lives have been different? Mourn losses to let go of past.
- What is a fantasy they hold for themselves for the future? What would it look like? What would they like for themselves?
- How will they know when they have integrated the effects of the abuse?
- What strategies and methods of coping can the group members adopt to achieve those goals?

Summarize Discussion in Terms of the Previous Questions

Relaxation Exercise

Check-Out

Impact of Childhood Sexual Abuse Questionnaire

Please rate the extent to which you believe the following statements are a result of the sexual abuse you experienced as a child.

1	2	3	4	5
great extent	moderate extent	somewhat	minor extent	not at all

Interpersonal

1. I feel isolated.	1	2	3	4	5
2. I feel different from others.	1	2	3	4	5
3. I don't trust others.	1	2	3	4	5
4. I don't trust men.	1	2	3	4	5
5. I don't trust women.	1	2	3	4	5
6. I have difficulty interacting with others.	1	2	3	4	5
7. I feel close to men.	1	2	3	4	5
8. I feel close to women.	1	2	3	4	5
9. I depend too much on others.	1	2	3	4	5
10. I cannot function at work.	1	2	3	4	5
11. I work too much.	1	2	3	4	5

Physical

1. I frequently suffer bodily aches and pains (e.g., headaches, soreness).	1	2	3	4	5
2. I feel sick when I do certain things. Describe:	1	2	3	4	5

_____

_____

Impact of Childhood Sexual Abuse Questionnaire *(continued)*

Emotional

1.	I become overly emotional.	1	2	3	4	5
2.	I don't feel anything.	1	2	3	4	5
3.	I don't feel good about myself.	1	2	3	4	5
4.	I feel helpless.	1	2	3	4	5
5.	I feel angry.	1	2	3	4	5
6.	I feel out of control at times.	1	2	3	4	5
7.	I feel powerful.	1	2	3	4	5
8.	I feel powerless.	1	2	3	4	5

Sexual

1.	I avoid sexual interactions.	1	2	3	4	5
2.	I engage in frequent sexual encounters.	1	2	3	4	5
3.	I'm confused about my sexuality.	1	2	3	4	5
4.	My sexual preference is a result of the abuse.	1	2	3	4	5

Family.

1.	I have good relations with my family of origin.	1	2	3	4	5
2.	I am estranged from my family of origin.	1	2	3	4	5
3.	I can talk openly with family members.	1	2	3	4	5
4.	My parents are divorced.	1	2	3	4	5

Impact of Childhood Sexual Abuse Questionnaire *(continued)*

5.	I prefer not to marry.	1	2	3	4	5
6.	I prefer not to have children.	1	2	3	4	5
7.	I am divorced.	1	2	3	4	5
8.	I am overprotective of my children.	1	2	3	4	5
9.	I have not developed adequate parenting skills.	1	2	3	4	5
10.	I work hard to be a good parent.	1	2	3	4	5

How would your life have been different if you had not been sexually abused?

_____

_____

_____

_____

_____

_____

_____

_____

_____

_____

_____

SOME DEFENSES THAT YOU MAY HAVE USED IN THE PAST (AND MAY STILL BE USING) TO HELP YOU COPE. CAN YOU IDENTIFY OTHERS?

Minimizing	Pretending it wasn't that bad.
Rationalizing	Explaining away the abuse: "He was drunk."
Denying	Pretending it didn't happen.
Forgetting	All of it or parts.
Splitting	Two different feeling states, e.g., good-bad, no gray, opposite, unintegrated views. May seem at times as if you have "left your body."
Control	Avoid chaos at all costs, organized, may be adaptive unless too rigid. It may inhibit flexibility and compromise.
Chaos	Opposite of control, tends to generate crises that keep you too busy to feel.
Spacing out	Dissociation—you cut yourself off from pain this way, but also miss out on a lot.
Hypervigilance	Always on guard.
Humor	Protects by distancing.
Workaholic	Protects by distancing, avoids feelings.
Escape	Fantasy life replaces reality.
Self-Mutilation	Control over experience of pain.
Suicide	Allows one to be in final control.
Eating disorders	Thinness to avoid growing into a woman's body, or obesity to keep one safe and unattractive.
Substance Abuse and Other Addictions	Numbs the pain, anesthesia.
Avoiding Intimacy	Safety.
Compulsive Sex	Search for the physical.

SESSION 6:
FAMILY DYNAMICS

Rationale

The family is the first model for intimacy in relationships. Survivors are frequently beset with a myriad of emotions regarding the family, from attachment and loyalty to anger and a sense of abandonment and betrayal. Some family members may have been, or are currently, very supportive, while others continue to deny the incest and to blame the victim. Disclosure of incest within the family system may have explosive effects with ramifications for future relationships. Each survivor must consider his/her individual experiences within his/her own family.

Relationships within sexually abusive families are frequently characterized by overly permeable, diffuse internal boundaries and overly rigid, isolating external boundaries. Family members learn that all significant needs can be met only within the family. The family unit becomes socially, psychologically, and physically isolated from the outside community.

Maddock and Larson (1995) present the view that incest is primarily a distortion of the sexual dimension of family experience. This experience arises from a combination of four equally influential variables:

- *Intrapsychic influences,* such as the internalized conflicts of family members regarding sexuality
- *Relational misbalances* between family members with regard to power/control, communication, or interpersonal boundary violations
- *Developmental variables,* including adaptation to change within the family system and role confusion
- *Situational factors,* such as availability of opportunity or a decrease in inhibition due to substance abuse (Maddock and Larson, 1995, pp. 72-73)

Two types of families are often described. The chaotic family system, frequently viewed as the characteristic sexually abusive family, is associated with limited education and low socioeconomic status, substance abuse, and lack of parental supervision. The "normal" appearing family is typified by the traditional model of father as head of household, liaison to the outside world. The internal structure of the family, however, is unstable and lacks emotional energy to adequately nurture its members. The children are often left to cope as best they can and are expected to assume caretaking roles. Such a role can be helping mother run the household or providing emotional and sexual sustenance for the father. Both types of families tend to be secretive, isolated, and in denial of reality. Parenting is inadequate, and violence or threat of violence may exist. Humor is minimal, while sarcasm and criticism are prevalent (Trepper and Barrett, 1989; Maddock and Larson, 1995).

Goals and Objectives

1. Understand the role of each family member and family patterns of behavior.
2. Become aware of conflicting emotions in regard to family of origin.
3. Understand the experience of incest in terms of family dynamics.
4. Discuss issues of blame, responsibility, and protection.
5. Grieve for lost image of the "perfect family."
6. Discuss issues of confrontation and forgiveness in terms of each member's own needs and experience.

Materials

Photographs of family; genograms; weekly evaluation questionnaires.

Procedure

Check-In

Questions to Guide Discussion

Raise questions for each member to answer:

- What was your family of origin like? What was it like for you to grow up in that system? What role did each member play? What was your role? What should have been the roles?
- What is your current family like? How is it similar to/different from your family of origin? What is your role today?

- What would your family have been like if there had been no incest?
- How has the experience of incest affected your forming a family today?
- How does your family understand your experience of incest? If you have not confronted your family, what would be some of your expectations, fears, and goals in telling them? Is it important for you to confront them? What would forgiveness mean? Is it possible? If you have confronted them, what has happened since then?

The use of family photographs and/or genograms may be helpful in eliciting memories and different emotions about the various family members.

Summarize Discussion in Terms of Previous Questions

Relaxation Exercise

Check-Out

Case Example

Diane is a forty-five-year-old married female of Irish-American heritage. She initially presented for treatment due to problems with an adopted daughter, a passive husband, and overly intrusive in-laws. At that time, she suffered severe anxiety attacks and depression. She felt unsupported and unheard within her family.

Diane came from a large family of nine children and was the eldest female. She describes her mother as emotionally absent and depressed and her father as a hardworking man who tried his best. Diane reports that her mother often became angry at and resentful of her, treating her very differently from her younger siblings. Diane was required to assume many of her mother's daily responsibilities as she grew older, and she soon took to mothering the younger siblings as well.

Her mother's neglect, and her own immobilizing depression, provided the conditions that allowed Diane to be sexually abused by her next-door neighbor over a period of five years, from the age of seven until the age of twelve. Her mother would encourage her to be friendly to the neighbor, literally pushing her over to his house to visit, run errands, etc. No amount of resistance on Diane's part persuaded her mother to let her stay home. Diane's attempts to tell her mother of the abuse went unheard and disbelieved. She received no protection or support within her own home and felt powerless to stop it on her own.

A stay-at-home and involved mother, Diane took great pride in raising two handicapped children and three adopted children. The family lived for seventeen years in a two-family home, with her in-laws occupying the other side. She describes her in-laws as controlling, verbally abusive, socially retarded, and nasty. Frequent conflicts erupted within and between the two households, with the mother-in-law becoming increasingly abusive to her own husband, as well as Diane's family.

When Diane's daughter began displaying signs of an eating disorder, Diane blamed it on her mother-in-law, and she finally decided to put an end to the abuse of her family. With an acrimonious separation, the two families parted, and Diane and her family began to build their own lives and relationships anew. This process created its own set of problems.

A recurrent theme was identified as Diane became involved in the group and began to discuss her role in, and feelings about, her family of origin and her husband's family. It became apparent that Diane's experience of her self within relationships was characterized by disregard and unmet needs. In the past, her husband's passivity and dependence on his family of origin had caused him to align himself with them to appease them, often at her expense. After the families separated, he became quite depressed and withdrawn, with communication between the couple reduced to a minimum. Again she experienced feelings of being shut out and disregarded. Connections between the childhood experience of being unheard and the similarity to her adult experiences were articulated within the group. For one of the first times in her life, Diane was able to experience what it felt like to be *heard* and *understood*.

SESSION 7:
SEXUALITY AND INTIMACY

Rationale

The correlation between a history of incest and its effect on varying aspects of sexuality, such as body perception, reproduction, sexual preference, sexual lifestyle, and sexual functioning, has been substantiated by recent research in this area (Maltz, 1991; Tharinger, 1990; Westerlund, 1992). It has been proposed that sexual abuse can result in the failure to complete normal developmental tasks in the psychosexual domain; consequently, abused children may be prematurely forced into the phallic stage of development (Kempe and Kempe, 1984). Finkelhor and Browne (1985) suggest that traumatic sexualization is a process in which a child's sexuality is shaped in developmentally inappropriate ways, resulting in inappropriate repertoires of sexual behavior and distorted cognitions about his/her own sexuality. Almost all clinical studies have shown later sexual problems among many child sexual abuse victims (e.g., difficulty with arousal, vaginismus, and flashbacks during sex, sexual guilt, sexual anxiety, and low sexual self-esteem). These difficulties can include, for example, a significant decrease in sexual desire, numbing or constriction during the arousal stage, and/or an inability to achieve orgasm. Additionally, survivors' interpersonalized interactions may become sexualized (e.g., suggestive, flirtatious) in nonsexual situations. This may be seen as the intrusion of sexually related issues into what is not inherently a sexual interaction. Therapeutic assistance is generally necessary to address distorted sexuality development and beliefs. It is important to view the sexual problems of survivors of incest in the context of their experiences and to restructure these dysfunctional assumptions and beliefs.

Goals and Objectives

1. Become aware of connections between sexual dysfunction and incest.
2. Help survivors overcome problematic thoughts and cognitions regarding their sexual dysfunction (self-blame, guilt, anger, and fear).

3. Enable survivors to regain control over their sexuality, to understand and validate sexuality and sexual preferences.
4. Discuss partner issues (choice of partner, similarity or dissimilarity to perpetrator, partner's feelings and expectations, communication).

Procedure

Check-In

Questions for Discussion

Raise questions for each member to answer:

- What is normal sexuality (physical, emotional, cognitive components, erotic function, self-esteem, intimacy, trust)?
- What have your sexual experiences been like? What have the aftereffects of those experiences been?
- If you had not been sexually abused as a child, how do you think your sexuality would have been different?
- What does incest teach about sexuality (e.g., sex life not your own, something that is done to you; sex as power, obligation, affection)?
- How are sexuality and intimacy interrelated and affected by incest experience?
- How can the effects of sexual abuse be separated from your present sexuality (awareness, recognizing own needs, setting limits, reconstruction of understanding about sexuality)?
- How does your partner understand your experiences? How can you successfully communicate your needs/feelings to your partner?*

---

*Maltz (1991) recommends a series of activities directed toward reducing negative associations to sexual interactions and enhancing sexual healing. She suggests exercises for relearning touch. These exercises are directed toward increasing relaxation and nonsexual touch, building safety within an intimate relationship, initiating and guiding intimate contact, increasing body awareness, and pleasuring self and partner. One example is an exercise that allows the individual to practice initiating and declining sex. The purpose of this is to "improve communication skills, increase empathy and reduce pressure regarding expressing interest in sexual activity" (p. 294).

- What options do you have to help improve your view of sexuality and sexual behaviors? How much of that is in your control?
- Have sexual relations ever been pleasurable and nonexploitive? What enabled you to reach that point? Is pleasurable sex a possibility for survivors? How can that be achieved? What would have to happen to have a positive sexual experience?

It is important to discuss the meanings and application of the "safe sex" concepts.

Summarize Discussion in Terms of Previous Questions

Relaxation Exercise

Check-Out

Case Example

Loretta was a twenty-nine-year-old female referred for treatment by her gynecologist due to sexual dysfunction. Since first engaging in sexual activity as a teenager, Loretta had suffered severe vaginismus. The persistent involuntary contraction of the perineal muscles prevented any but the most painful vaginal penetration. Loretta and her husband of eight years discussed having children but could not overcome this physical obstacle.

Loretta, the only female, was the youngest of three children from an intact, argumentative, Catholic family. Father was reported to be a recovering alcoholic and had been diagnosed as manic-depressive. Mother was the disciplinarian. Loretta reported that both her parents worked long hours when she was a child, although her father had difficulty maintaining employment and gradually withdrew into himself. Loretta was expected to complete all the household chores. She denied any history of intrafamilial sexual abuse.

Loretta presented with depressed mood, anxiety, difficulty sleeping, and irritability. She reported an absence of sexual relations with her husband in recent months but did admit to an extramarital affair with a co-worker, although normal sexual intercourse was not achieved. Through an exploration of the development of the vaginismus, it was revealed that she had never had any real sexual relationship or normal intercourse. Her first sexual encounter was at the age of twelve, when a friend's brother raped her. Loretta remembered little about this event, other than that it was forced on her against her will. A second encounter also resulted in forced intercourse. As Loretta began to discuss her early sexual experiences, she realized that all were forced upon her until she met and married her husband.

Loretta began to explore the impact of the rapes on her emerging sexual identity. For the first time, she was able to connect the use of force with the lack of enjoyment she experienced during sex and the severe vaginismus she suffered. This realization opened the way for her to discuss her fears and her confusion regarding her sexuality and her intimate relationships. The group's discussions of their own sexual behaviors, beliefs, and attitudes enabled Loretta to express the feelings of shame and damage that she had held on to since the first rape. Similar experiences and emotions within the group fostered the reinterpretation of her role in the experience as a twelve-year-old. She began to develop a new understanding of her adult sexuality. Gradually, Loretta was able to identify and regain control over her own sexual needs, and for the first time in her marriage, she engaged in successful intercourse.

SESSION 8:
PROCESSING MEMORIES

Rationale

The controversy over the validity and impact of recalled memories of child sexual abuse has direct implications for the therapeutic treatment of adult survivors of abuse. On one side of the argument is the belief in the existence of delayed recall of traumatic memory. On the other side are those who suggest that recovered memories are the result of misinformation and suggestibility. There is general consensus from both corners, however, that the recall of traumatic events is a complex, and at times conflicting, area of concern.

Memory has been an area of research for decades; recent studies have supported and replicated the basic principles proposed by earlier research. Today it is understood that memory should not be considered a passive, static videotape of experience but rather a process that actively selects and constructs incoming perceptions (Pope and Brown, 1996). Ross (1989) has expressed the view that recollections of early life are processed as "an integrated set of related representations of actions . . . that life's experiences can be processed and superimposed upon the corpus of one's [early memories]" (p. 281). Citing Loftus (1988), Pope and Brown (1996) explain that "new life experiences, new information, and the very process of remembering itself can change what we have represented in memory, and, in some models of memory, erase and replace prior memory traces with new, sometimes inaccurate, information" (p. 36). Autobiographical memory is an example of the memory of episodes in a person's life reflecting that person's personal narrative of who he/she is, and what he/she has experienced. This memory may take on different meanings when it is integrated into prior knowledge, a set of related representations, or cognitive schemata.

Various factors may influence how memory is retained in the short term and transferred into long-term storage. The individual's state of arousal, attention to the event, and emotional state influence the likelihood of later recall. In addition, repetition or rehearsal of the information, and structural properties specific to that information, increases the likelihood of transfer into long-term memory. Factors in the person's interpersonal environment have also been found to affect the ability to recall what has happened. The presence of social support at the time of the event increases the likelihood of remembering that event (Pope and Brown, 1996).

What emerges from the study of memory is the understanding that what people report they remember is influenced by the salience of the material, how it has been stored, and how it has been retrieved (recognized, recalled, or recollected). The validity of those memories therefore depends on the characteristics, context, and personal meaning of the event. It is a version of what has happened that is mediated by many different intervening variables. It is believed that emotional events may be remembered differently from neutral or commonplace events. These memories have been described as detailed, accurate, and not prone to error.

Implantation of false autobiographical memory has been of particular concern since the concept of a *false memory syndrome* was first discussed (False Memory Syndrome Foundation [FMSF], 1992). Proponents of false memory doubt the validity of recovered memories of childhood abuse. They assert that human memory is subject to inaccuracy, fabrication, confusion, suggestion, and alteration (Loftus, 1993) and that therapists may be (unwittingly) implanting suggestions, or may be overzealous in their effort to uncover "repressed" memories. The susceptibility of adults and children to misinformation has been studied extensively by memory researchers, often with conflicting results (Ceci and Bruck, 1995; Loftus, 1993; Pezdek and Roe, 1994; Zaragoza, 1991). Current evidence refutes the view that memory related to trauma is easily subject to suggestion. It appears that memories associated with strong affect are less susceptible to suggestion (Christianson, 1992); that central details of memory remain intact even while a small portion of memory may be misrepresented (Pope and Brown, 1996); that common events are more easily replaced with pseudomemories than uncommon events; and that resistance or vulnerability to suggestion are influenced by age, actual experience rather than observation of an event, and the degree of social support available (Pezdek and Roe, 1994). Readers are referred to Doris (1991) for a comprehensive treatment of this subject.

Repression, the phenomenon that prevents someone from remembering an event that can cause pain or suffering, has also been studied extensively to explain how traumatic experiences might be forgotten and later recalled. This theoretical term has been replaced with the more behaviorally descriptive term of *delayed memory,* or *delayed recall* (Pope and Brown, 1996). Delayed recall has been associated with the concept of state-dependent remembering, in the belief that "memories acquired in one state are accessible mainly in that state, but are dissociated or not available for recall in an alternate state" (Bower, 1981, p. 130). This theory connects the affect and content of an event and proposes that memory recall is strengthened by mood congruity (Alpert, 1995). It has been suggested that state dependent memory is highly correlated with early abusive experiences; that is, memory becomes more state dependent with increased incidence of abuse. The individual will then recall these events only when reminded by cues of a specific emotional and contextual nature (Dalenberg et al., 1995). It may be the dissociation that best explains the delayed recall or temporary loss of memory for traumatic events. Until the person is exposed to specific, disinhibiting retrieval cues, neurological and cognitive factors may inhibit conscious access to traumatic memory (Yates and Nasby, 1993).

It is believed that chronic, severe childhood trauma may permanently alter neurological structures and functions that integrate memory and affect the way that memory is stored and retrieved (van der Kolk and Saporta, 1991; Wylie, 1993). It has been noted that memory storage and retrieval may be affected by the degree of emotional arousal, and may be associated with different parts of the brain. Neurohormones released into the brain at the time of trauma may enhance the consolidation and storage of these emotionally laden events (Cahill et al., 1994). Verified reports of fragmented memory for trauma have been associated with deficits in the ambient cortisol levels in the brain (Yehuda et al., 1995). Changes to the limbic system and amygdala of trauma survivors, when compared to control subjects, have also been shown (van der Kolk and Saporta, 1991). Emotionally laden memories may be stored in these brain structures. Preliminary research also suggests that there are neurochemical correlates of certain kinds of intense emotional experiences (Putnam and Tricket, 1993).

It also has been hypothesized that after repeated traumatization the brain may become so overwhelmed by negative arousal that cognitive memory and emotion are, in effect, severed. (The emotional sensations related to trauma may then be remembered through a different memory, either as bodily sensations or visual images.) This may help explain the occurrence of flashbacks or body memories without conscious recollection. Freyd (1996) suggests that there may be an evolutionary adaptive function to the phenomenon of delayed recall of traumatic memory, which makes these memories inaccessible to conscious recollection until adulthood. Dependency on the adult for survival makes it maladaptive for the child to recognize the adult's betrayal of trust. Recollection of the abuse and betrayal of trust can occur only when the risk of survival is minimized or nonexistent.

What does the clinician take away from these studies? In the first place, comprehension of traumatic memory requires a "complex model that integrates understanding of neural phenomena, the meaning of the trauma for the individual, and the relationship of the traumatic experience to the overall personal context" (Koss, Tromp, and Tharan, 1995, as cited in Pope and Brown, 1996, p. 58). When applying this information therapeutically, professionals "need to be cautious in generalizing from the limited current findings, and to be clear that each person will have had a different capacity to store the memory, as well as unique abilities to forget and remember it" (Pope and Brown, 1996, p. 59).

Lindsay and Briere (1997) raise the practical question of whether it is helpful to encourage memory retrieval in therapy or in self-help groups. Based on rigorous research demonstrating the beneficial effects of attention to, and desensitization of, abuse memories, these authors conclude that "it is reasonable to hypothesize that adult survivors of remembered childhood trauma can also benefit from verbally exploring traumatic memories" (p. 640).

It is not memory recovery, per se, but rather memory recovery in a context that includes suggestive influences and misinformation that is of more concern. Memory recovery may occur naturally as a function of good psychotherapy that lessens the need for defensive strategies which have reduced the distress associated with remembering overwhelming events (Lindsay and Briere, 1997, p. 641).

A partial reconstructive perspective appears to be more reasonable than expecting either a literal reproduction or major alteration in adult memory. It is important to ascertain the client's basic level of reality testing, as well as the general level of autobiographic memory. Current history and functioning, coping strategies, and dissociative mechanisms may provide insight into past patterns of memory storage and retrieval. The goal of therapy is not memory recovery but rather an exploration of the meaning of the memories for the individual to allow the experience to be interpreted and understood by the adult survivor.

When working with survivors, it is important to avoid the assumption that a client who cannot remember his/her childhood is repressing traumatic memories. It is essential to avoid asking suggestive or leading questions. Mirroring back what the client has already stated, multisource corroboration, videotaping, self-monitoring, and allowing the client to lead the way can be useful techniques to avoid these pitfalls. Previously inaccessible memories may resurface spontaneously as defensive strategies are replaced with alternative coping strategies and new understanding of the experience. It is important that the survivor decide what his/her memories might mean. The therapist should be careful to neither construct nor debase the memory for the survivor.

This controversy begs the question of whether determining the absolute truth or falsehood is always a necessary precondition for treatment. It is important to consider what the negative results of incorrectly believing the abuse disclosure would be, as compared to the benefit of correctly rejecting the beliefs as false (Briere, 1989). Disbelief may perpetuate the denial surrounding the occurrence of the sexual abuse and may cause the client continued harm. It is always important to understand the meaning of these memories for the individual.

Goals and Objectives

1. Facilitate adult understanding of childhood memories, flashbacks, and body memories.
2. Understand personal meaning of memories within own life experience.

3. Develop strategies to aid in intrusive symptoms of memory recall.
4. Reconnect memory with its associated affect.

Materials

Photographs, paper and pencil, and floor plans; weekly evaluation questionnaires.

Procedure

Check-In

Introduce the Evening's Topic—Processing of Memories

Many clients are fearful that new memories or flashbacks may arise unexpectedly, severely interfering with their everyday functioning. Normalize the possibility that new memories of the abuse may be overwhelming at times. Suggest ways that they can contain the memories until they are able to work on them. Strategies may include scheduling a specific time to work on the memories, decreasing the amount of stress they are experiencing in their lives, particularly in an intensive period, and visualizing the memories as "locked in a box and stored on the shelf."

Questions for Discussion

Raise questions for each member to answer:

- Is it important to recover all memory of the abuse?
- What fears/expectations do you have about remembering?
- What purpose might repressing memories have served?
- What would it mean to you if you never remembered more than you know right now?

Discuss techniques for retrieving memories. These may include using childhood photographs, drawing out floor plans of the childhood home, mentally walking through the house, and talking to other family members and childhood friends.

Discuss strategies for containment of unsolicited memory:

- What could they do when memories come unexpectedly and inconveniently?
- What are some coping strategies to contain these flashbacks and unexpected memories? (For example, one strategy is to visualize putting the memories away under lock and key, or buried in a deep pit, to be taken out only when the person is able to deal with them.)

Summarize Discussion

Practice Relaxation Exercise

Check-Out

SESSIONS 9-13:
EXPLORING THE MEANING—
UNSTRUCTURED SESSIONS

Rationale

This provides the opportunity for group members to raise issues that they consider important, current, and in need of further detailed discussion. It empowers the group to take charge, to take responsibility for their own actions, address their needs, and, perhaps, assume new roles. Group process, dynamics, and interactional patterns can be addressed in greater detail at this time.

Goals and Objectives

1. Discuss issues raised by the group.
2. Transfer more responsibility for the group to the group members themselves.
3. Continue discussion of issues raised in previous sessions.
4. Facilitate further integration of cognitions, memories, and affect.

Procedure

Check-In

During the check-in, issues generally arise that provide a focus for the group discussion. If this fails to occur, encourage the group to raise issues they would like to talk about. The role of the facilitators at this time is to monitor group discussion, mirror what has been said in the group, and maintain a safe forum for the group's discussion.

Practice Relaxation Exercises

Check-Out

SESSIONS 14-15:
TOWARD TERMINATION—MAKING SENSE OF IT ALL

Rationale

As the fifteen weeks draw to a close, it is important to begin discussing reactions to the pending termination. Clients may be experiencing feelings of loss, rejection, abandonment, anxiety, sadness, or even relief. These themes will also be touched upon in each of the next two sessions.

Goals and Objectives

1. Review progress over the past fifteen weeks.
2. Discuss future options.
3. Evaluate goal attainment.
4. Discuss ways of continuing the healing process.

Procedure

Check-In

Discuss Termination Issues

Remind the group that this is the second to last session. Some common feelings may include abandonment—"You are leaving me just as I am beginning to trust"—and fear of relationships—"It is unsafe to develop new relationships because they end." What is each group member thinking and feeling about the group coming to an end?

Review Each Member's Progress

Review progress over the past twelve to fifteen weeks. Remind everyone of goals set in the first session. Have they achieved their goals? If not, why not? If so, what was useful to them? What might be some future goals? Each group member should be encouraged to evaluate his/her own functioning and progress.

Continuing the Healing Process

How might they continue the healing process? What does healing mean for them? How will they know when it is resolved? What will it look like? What will they do? How will they get there?

Plan for Last Session

How would they like the group to end? Some groups prefer an informal session with food and drink to celebrate the completion of this group's work. Others may prefer remaining with the structure and format of previous sessions.

Practice Relaxation Exercises

Check-Out

Chapter 7

Special Topics

ETHNICITY AND SEXUAL ABUSE

Ethnicity has been defined as a cultural orientation encompassing common traditions and customs that is shared by a large group of people (Barbee, 1991). This definition promotes an understanding of an individual's heritage that extends beyond the consideration of race alone, an important dimension in the understanding of an individual's mental health. It is important in both assessment and intervention of psychological difficulties.

In the past few years, increasing attention has been paid to the relationship between ethnicity and sexual abuse. The way the culture's values, norms, attitudes, and expectations regarding sexual behaviors influence the person's attributions about and understanding of the sexually abusive experience, and the meaning they assign to it, has been a special focus of many studies (Mennen, 1994). Of equal importance is the understanding of the connection between racism and sexism and violence against women, particularly women of color. Of interest is that little, if any, research has been conducted on ethnic differences of incidence and effect among sexually abused males.

Barbee (1991) presents the argument that racist and patriarchal attitudes prevalent in the United States have contributed to the devaluation of women of color and have promoted the use of violence against them. For example, four stereotypic images (the mammy, the matriarch, the welfare mother, and the Jezebel) contribute to the view of the African-American woman as an independent, sexually promiscuous breeder whose body is expendable. This view has been used by some to justify acts of violence against women of color.

Wilson (1994) argues that the role of the black male in society contributes to violence against women of color. The black male does not receive respect or have power within society due to the constraints of racism. Instead, according to Wilson, he compensates by seeking it within his own community. The abuse of power and demand for respect at home is believed by some to be a justifiable outlet valve for the stresses caused by racism. There may be tacit acceptance of this view within the community that then interacts with the taboo of talking about the abuse. Revealing the secrets of the community is viewed as betrayal and disloyalty. Male authority is therefore achieved at the expense of female equality.

Wyatt (1990) reported significant ethnic differences regarding the short-term reaction to abuse and in women's attitudes toward men in adulthood. For African-American women, short-term effects were associated with more severe contact abuse experiences. Growing into womanhood in a race-conscious society may increase the self-conscious awareness of the stereotype of the black female. Due to historical and social criteria, the African-American woman may not view herself as a believable victim of sexual abuse. She may be less likely to disclose the abuse than her white peers, thereby increasing the cumulative impact of the sexual victimization and the risk for revictimization (Wyatt, Notgrass, and Gordon, 1995). This may also be true of the Hispanic community, in which strong traditional values against discussion of personal family matters outside the family may explain low rates of disclosure found among Hispanic children (Becerra and Iglehart, 1995).

Contradictory findings have been reported about the incidence of abuse among different ethnic/racial groups, the specifics of the abuse, and the symptoms related to the abuse (Mennen, 1994). Ethnic differences have been found among African-American, Latino, and white abused children in regard to age of victim, family income, type and severity of abuse, and perpetrator. Urban, latency-age African-American girls whose mothers did not complete high school were found to have the highest rate and most serious consequences of abuse (Hampton, 1987). When compared with white women, African-American women reported more severe levels of abuse and greater use of force, resulting in extreme upset with greater long-term effects (Russell, Schurman, and Trocki, 1988).

The combined findings indicate that racial/ethnic differences do exist in sexual abuse trauma, although the nature of influence remains inconclusive. What is clear is that environmental conditions such as poverty, racial and ethnic discrimination, and economic stress contribute to the occurrence of sexual abuse.

Some directions emerging from current research highlight the importance of ethnicity in the treatment of sexual abuse. Mennen (1994), in a study of 134 racially diverse girls, found that the racial/ethnic differences that do exist may have implications for treatment. For example, the possibility of penetration may have an important meaning and increase the likelihood of serious symptoms in Latino victims due to the importance of virginity in this population. Levels of depression were also affected by ethnic background. Higher depression scores were associated with earlier onset of abuse and abuse by a relative, conditions found more often in the Latino sample (Sanders-Philips et al., 1995). African-American women tended to seek more internal reasons, such as their physical development, as the cause for their victimization (Wyatt, 1985, 1986). Increased maternal support occurred more frequently in the African-American subgroup and has been associated with more positive outcomes. These preliminary findings indicate that a person's cultural/racial/ethnic background provides a framework within which meaning is assigned to experience. The implications for treatment are evident: "An understanding of ethnic differences in psychological functioning, and identification of the determinants of differences is important to the development of successful interventions" (Sanders-Philips et al., 1995, p. 692).

Barbeė (1991) advocates the use of different approaches when treating clients with ethnic backgrounds different from the Euro-American model. These approaches are based upon the understanding of a culture that places importance on interrelatedness and interdependence, as well as a reluctance to share problems outside the family/friends network (p. 162). Culturally appropriate intervention would recognize that African-American women, for example, value this family/friend network, have been socialized not to talk about their problems, and usually do not seek treatment. Developing a rapport that understands their distrust of the system is critical. It is also essential to involve concerned family and friends in treatment and to strengthen the development of support networks.

Women need to be reeducated about the effects of the abuse, the likelihood of revictimization, and sexual abuse prevention measures. Education should occur within the context of the individual's relationships, as well as the social and economic environment in which she lives (Wyatt, Notgrass, and Gordon, 1995).

CONFRONTATION

Cameron (1994) provides a complete summary of the pros and cons of survivors confronting their abusers. Many authors have addressed the issues relevant to abuser confrontation, viewing it as both empowering and painful for the survivor. Key issues concerning the process of confrontation include the decision whether to confront, deciding when and how to confront, and dealing with the aftermath of the confrontation. Recommendations have been made concerning assessing motivations, preparation, and possible outcomes prior to the confrontation (Bass and Davis, 1988).

The issue of whether confrontation is essential for full recovery has been considered. Meiselman (1990) advocated for those who choose not to confront: "In no case should the therapist insist on confrontation or hold it up to the client as a criterion for success in therapy" (p. 168). Only the survivor can decide to confront the abuser, and he/she will do so when/if ready. Alternatives to direct conflict that may better serve the survivor include letter writing, the empty chair technique, and role-playing.

Should the survivor choose confrontation, Herman and Schatzow (1984) have defined clear parameters. These include an extensive preparation period, during which the survivor explores motivation, develops a supportive alliance with the therapist, and increases understanding of individual and family dynamics prior to the actual exercise. The survivor should be prepared for any eventuality, be able to dictate the conditions, and be ready to process the event after it has taken place (Cameron, 1994).

McBride and Markos (1994) have identified additional sources of difficulty that may arise in the treatment of survivors of sexual abuse. These problems may stem from initial complications in diagnosis or from difficulties within the client's or therapist's own experiences.

PSYCHIATRIC DISORDERS, CHEMICAL DEPENDENCY, AND SEXUAL ABUSE

Clients frequently present for treatment with a multitude of concerns seemingly unrelated to the abuse. They often do not identify themselves as survivors of sexual abuse, even if they are aware of that fact. Psychiatric disorders such as depression, anxiety, eating disorders, substance abuse, and sexual difficulties, to name a few, often mask the history of abuse.

An example of this is often found with women in treatment for chemical dependency. Past studies have reported high rates of incest and other forms of sexual and family violence among drug-dependent women (Ladwig and Andersen, 1991). Addressing the issue of abuse in chemically dependent individuals may be fundamental to their recovery. Sexual abuse is often treated as a secondary, rather than primary, issue in treatment (Courtois, 1988). It has been suggested that substance abuse may have developed as a way to deal with past and present stressors, including the sexual abuse (Ladwig and Andersen, 1991). The abuse of substances is often an attempt to anesthetize the feelings of abuse and may indicate that the survivor is having extreme difficulty tolerating those feelings. Remembering and reexperiencing feelings associated with the sexual abuse trauma has been found to be a major precipitant of relapse (Wadsworth, Spampneto, and Halbrook, 1995). The high rate of relapse might be due to inadequate treatment of the specific needs of these individuals with regard to past history of abuse. Substance abuse may occur because of the sense of power imbued and the concomitant decrease in anxiety. Alternative coping strategies must be developed concurrently with sexual abuse treatment so that the individual may remain sober and avoid relapse while still confronting the painful experience.

For many of the same reasons that group therapy is the preferred treatment for sexual abuse, it is also the treatment of choice for chemical dependency (Blume, 1985). Feelings of isolation and alienation can be reduced within the group as new supports and coping strategies are developed. The group facilitators may wish to include this topic for discussion at various points during the fifteen-week program.

TRANSFERENCE AND COUNTERTRANSFERENCE

Survivors themselves often present roadblocks during treatment. Behaviors that were adaptive and protective while the abuse was occurring may interfere with the establishment of the therapeutic alliance. Interpersonal functioning is one domain that has been most directly affected by the abuse. Denial, fear, resistance, and reluctance may also interfere with the sexual abuse work (McBride and Markos, 1994). The client may also symbolically reenact the past, the transference, within the therapeutic relationship. Transference has been defined as "the unconscious repetition in a current relationship of patterns, thoughts, feelings, expectations and responses that originated in important early relationships" (Pearlman and Saakvitne, 1995, p. 100). Survivors of childhood sexual abuse are often caught in a "double bind," in which the "positive aspects of relatedness are viewed as necessarily accompanied by pain" (Waites, 1993, p. 184). One can expect transference reactions in the areas of self-capacities, frame of reference issues (the client's fundamental identity and worldview), and the client's psychological needs and schemata (Pearlman and Saakvitne, 1995).

The following is an excerpt from a letter received from a group participant after the group had terminated. One of this woman's central issues concerned her relationship with her mother, whom she perceived as a wealthy, uncaring, vain woman who was unable to nurture her as a child:

> I hope you will not be hurt by the following comment. I can't speak for the other group members, but I found your wardrobe very off-putting. You are clearly in a position of authority, and your clothes emphasized to me that you are privileged compared to the rest of us [i.e., the incest survivors]. I don't think I am unusual in distrusting people who are different from me, and your shoes and clothes made you seem

different. I have read that a therapist is well-advised to dress inconspicuously, and I think that's true . . .

Therapists themselves may be the source of difficulty when working with this population, and they need to identify, tolerate, and understand their own responses. These countertransferential responses can stem from insufficient training in the treatment of sexual abuse, resulting in knowledge and skill deficits. These deficits may then translate into a failure to ask about the abuse trauma and incorrect diagnosis and treatment (McBride and Markos, 1994).

In addition, an unresolved personal history of abuse may underlie a therapist's reluctance to delve more directly into the client's problems, thereby impeding the course of treatment. It is imperative that the therapist's own attitudes, feelings, and personal reactions be fully explored prior to engaging in treatment of sexually abused clients.

Work with adult survivors of sexual abuse can be both exhilarating and demoralizing. Helping an individual come to terms with his/her past history while still moving ahead toward a satisfying life can be most rewarding. Yet, the therapist should also be prepared for the possible negative effects of this kind of treatment. The content of treatment may have a great impact on the therapist, particularly due to the isolating nature of psychotherapy.

Pearlman and Saakvitne (1995) have suggested that vicarious traumatization may also be a source of difficulty for the therapist. Therapists are frequently witnesses to the recall and reliving of the traumatic memories of abuse. Typical countertransferential responses can be expected as the therapist experiences a wide range of emotions and visceral reactions. Reactions to the client's pain may include feelings of helplessness, anger, and disillusionment (burnout), to name a few. Difficulty tolerating and containing these affective responses may be expressed in a blurring of boundaries (overinvestment), an attempt to distance oneself from the client (disengagement), action-oriented advocacy for clients, or full counteridentification resulting in vicarious traumatization of the therapist (Kluft, 1990; Price, 1994; Pearlman and Saakvitne, 1995). All of these responses may be detrimental to the therapeutic process.

One way to minimize the therapist's countertransferential reactions is to provide thorough training and supervision throughout the treatment. This training should include "a solid theoretical foundation that includes an understanding of the effect of psychological trauma, a relational perspective and attention to the issues of counter-transference and vicarious traumatization" (Pearlman and Saakvitne, 1995, p. 564). Therapy for the therapist may also be indicated.

PARTNERS

Healing after a traumatic experience such as childhood sexual abuse is often a prolonged period of emotional turmoil, with frequently changing states of consciousness and understanding. It affects not only the survivor but also the partner or significant other in his/her life. Marital discord is one long-term effect of childhood sexual abuse that has been documented by researchers (Jehu, 1988; Finkelhor, 1990; Firth, 1997). Psychological, interpersonal, and sexual problems exist for the partner, as well as for the survivor. The impairment of trust, fear of intimacy, and sexual dysfunction appear to be the most prevalent and pervasive effects of the abuse within relationships. Other potential abuse-related problems within this relationship have been suggested (Wilson and James, 1992; Chauncey, 1994; Firth, 1997) and may include conflicting needs; difficulty with spontaneity or unpredictability; anger, guilt, and shame; the process of the survivor's recovery; concerns about disclosure; and relationships with the extended family and/or children.

The effects of childhood sexual abuse on the partner, the impact of the survivor's therapy on the partner, and the role of the partner in the survivor's healing are emerging as important issues to consider in treatment. Marital therapy has been recommended as a necessary adjunct to individual therapy because focusing primarily on the survivor's abuse may obscure current relational functioning (Alexander, Neimeyer, and Follette, 1991; Bacon and Lein, 1996). "Changes in the survivor during psychotherapy, such as enhanced self-esteem, increased assertiveness, or a desire for reallocation of roles within their primary relationship, are considered to be progress, but may require that partners accept and adapt to these changes" (Bacon and Lein, 1996, pp. 3-4).

Bacon and Lein (1996) studied the effects of women's childhood sexual abuse on male partners and the couple relationship. They found that relationships which had been balanced while affect and/ or memory of the abuse was repressed became unbalanced and unpredictable, creating, in essence, an emotional roller-coaster ride for the partner. Despite this unsettling effect, the authors also found that these partners were committed to their relationships and were sources of strength that could be used in the survivor's healing.

Various approaches have been suggested as to how best to involve partners in the survivor's treatment. Firth (1997) identified sexual dysfunction, emotional problems, and interpersonal difficulties as the main targets for treatment of the survivor and partner; these can be addressed in individual, couple, group, and self-help therapies. The meaning of the abuse to both partners can be explored, education and information about the effects of abuse and the process of healing can be imparted, and relational and sexual dysfunction can be improved.

Group therapy for partners is seen as a necessary step in the healing process, although little is known about group processes and outcomes for the partner (Firth, 1997). Jehu (1988) provides one example of a group treatment program for male partners. Treatment goals for this group were identified as alleviation of feelings of difference and isolation from other men; mutual aid and support; and understanding, acceptance of, and adaptation to the problems and changes in victims. Exchange of information, development of coping skills, and the development of a framework for understanding their own reactions to sexual abuse were important outcomes of the group. Work with female partners of male victims may present additional problems, including addressing male gender socialization and attitudes toward male roles in society.

SUMMARY

Childhood sexual abuse is a problem that has reached extreme proportions in today's society. This childhood experience has been shown to influence the child's developing belief system and worldview. This subsequently may affect the adult's ability to function adaptively. Physical, emotional, interpersonal, and cognitive sequelae must be addressed, and understood, in the context of the adult's cognitive capacity, if the individual is to move beyond the impact of this traumatic experience.

Therapists continue to see increasing numbers of clients in their practices who report past sexual abuse. Unfortunately, as Alpert (1990) and Pope and Feldman-Summers (1992) noted, little formal training in the treatment of sexual abuse is incorporated into graduate programs. A gap has developed between a very evident need for specialized treatment and sufficiently trained resources to meet that need. This program is offered as a guideline that, hopefully, professionals and students alike can utilize to bridge that gap.

Appendix A

Needs Assessment Surveys

CSA NEEDS ASSESSMENT SURVEY: PROFESSIONALS

1. Please rate, using the scale below, (a) the extent to which women who have been involved in an incestuous relationship during childhood possess the following characteristics (left side) and (b) the extent to which they should possess these characteristics to achieve a healthier level of functioning (right side).

1	2	3	4	5
great		somewhat		not at all

currently possess		should possess
1 2 3 4 5	Recognize and express own feelings (e.g., anger, sadness, loss, joy)	1 2 3 4 5
1 2 3 4 5	Knowledgeable about incest/sexual abuse	1 2 3 4 5
1 2 3 4 5	Recognize and care for personal needs (emotional and physical)	1 2 3 4 5
1 2 3 4 5	Establish and maintain intimate interpersonal relationships	1 2 3 4 5
1 2 3 4 5	Communicate effectively	1 2 3 4 5
1 2 3 4 5	Aware of effects of sexual abuse and trauma	1 2 3 4 5
1 2 3 4 5	Able to trust others	1 2 3 4 5
1 2 3 4 5	Able to trust their own intuitions and perceptions	1 2 3 4 5
1 2 3 4 5	Recognize personal strengths and capabilities	1 2 3 4 5
1 2 3 4 5	Develop adaptive coping strategies	1 2 3 4 5

2. In your opinion, of the characteristics listed, which three are most important for these women to acquire to facilitate healthy functioning? Please rank these three characteristics in order of importance.

_____

_____

_____

CSA NEEDS ASSESSMENT SURVEY: CLIENTS

1. Please rate, using the scale below, (a) the extent to which you possess the following characteristics (left side) and (b) the extent to which you would like to acquire these characteristics to achieve a healthier level of functioning (right side).

currently possess		would like to acquire
1 2 3 4 5	I recognize and express my own feelings (e.g., anger, sadness, loss, joy).	1 2 3 4 5
1 2 3 4 5	I am knowledgeable about incest/ sexual abuse.	1 2 3 4 5
1 2 3 4 5	I recognize and care for my personal needs (emotional and physical).	1 2 3 4 5
1 2 3 4 5	I establish and maintain intimate interpersonal relationships.	1 2 3 4 5
1 2 3 4 5	I communicate effectively.	1 2 3 4 5
1 2 3 4 5	I am aware of the effects of sexual abuse and trauma.	1 2 3 4 5
1 2 3 4 5	I am able to trust others.	1 2 3 4 5
1 2 3 4 5	I am able to trust my own intuitions and perceptions.	1 2 3 4 5
1 2 3 4 5	I recognize my personal strengths and capabilities.	1 2 3 4 5
1 2 3 4 5	I can develop adaptive coping strategies.	1 2 3 4 5

2. In your opinion, of the characteristics listed, which three are most important for you to acquire for healthier functioning? Please rank these three characteristics in order of their importance.

Appendix B

Weekly Evaluation Questionnaire for Group Leaders

DATE _____   **SESSION #_____**   **TOPIC** _____

1. How would you rate the rapport in tonight's session?

| 1 | 2 | 3 | 4 | 5 |
| Excellent | | | | Poor |

2. What were the goals of tonight's session?

_____

_____

_____

3. How successful was the session in accomplishing tonight's goals?

| 1 | 2 | 3 | 4 | 5 |
| Very | | | | Not Successful |

4. If the goals were not met, why not?

_____

_____

_____

5. What was the most positive aspect of tonight's session?

_____

_____

_____

6. What was the least positive aspect of tonight's session?

_____

_____

_____

7. Did you change anything in tonight's session? ___Y   ___N

8. If so, what was changed?

_____

_____

_____

9. How could this session have been improved?

_____

_____

_____

10. Additional comments:

_____

_____

_____

_____

_____

Appendix C

Survivors of Childhood Sexual Abuse Program—Weekly Evaluation Questionnaire

DATE _____ **SESSION #**____ **TOPIC** _____

1. How helpful was this group for you?

        1   2   3
    extremely   somewhat   not at all

2. What did you find most helpful about the session?

    _____

    _____

    _____

3. To what extent did this group session help you feel less isolated?

        1   2   3
    great   somewhat   not at all

After participating in this group session:

4. Do you feel better equipped to discuss your incestuous experience with appropriate others?

___Y   ___N

5. Did you acquire additional information about the dynamics of sexual abuse?

___Y   ___N

6. Did you acquire new skills to help you deal more effectively with the effects of your incestuous experience on your current functioning?

___Y   ___N

7. Are you more aware of how your childhood experience has affected your current functioning?

___Y   ___N

8. To what extent did the group help you understand the mechanisms you used to cope with this experience?

1	2	3
great	somewhat	not at all

9. To what extent did participation in this session help you learn to recognize your personal, emotional, and physical needs?

1	2	3
great	somewhat	not at all

10. To what extent did this session teach you new ways of caring for yourself?

1	2	3
great	somewhat	not at all

11. To what extent did the session help you begin developing alternative behaviors that will lead to healthier functioning in your current life?

    1   2   3

  great   somewhat   not at all

12. How would you change this session if you could?

_____

_____

_____

13. What issues would you like to discuss in future sessions?

_____

_____

_____

14. How would you rate the quality of service provided?

    1   2   3   4

excellent   good   fair   poor

15. Did you get the type of service you wanted?

    1   2   3   4

  yes   generally   not really   not at all

16. Additional comments:

_____

_____

_____

_____

_____

_____

Appendix D

Survivors of Childhood Sexual Abuse Program—Evaluation Questionnaire

FINAL EVALUATION/THREE-MONTH FOLLOW-UP

1. How helpful was this group for you?

1	2	3
extremely	somewhat	not at all

2. What did you find most helpful about the group?

_____

_____

_____

_____

3. To what extent did this group help you feel less isolated?

1	2	3
great	somewhat	not at all

4. After participating in the group, do you feel better equipped to discuss your incestuous experience with appropriate others?

___Y   ___N

5. Did you acquire additional information about the dynamics of sexual abuse?

___Y   ___N

6. Did you acquire new skills to help you deal more effectively with the effects of your incestuous experience on your current functioning?

___Y   ___N

7. Are you more aware of how your childhood experience has affected your current functioning?

___Y   ___N

8. To what extent did the group help you understand the mechanisms you used to cope with this experience?

1	2	3
great	somewhat	not at all

9. To what extent did participation in this group help you learn to recognize your personal, emotional, and physical needs?

1	2	3
great	somewhat	not at all

10. To what extent did this group teach you new ways of caring for yourself?

1	2	3
great	somewhat	not at all

11. To what extent did the group help you begin developing alternative behaviors that will lead to healthier functioning in your current life?

1	2	3
great	somewhat	not at all

12. How would you change the group if you could?

_____

_____

_____

13. Would you be interested in continuing to participate in a group of this nature?

___Y   ___N

14. What issues would you like to discuss in future sessions/groups?

_____

_____

_____

15. To what extent were the group leaders successful in facilitating the group?

1	2	3
great	somewhat	not at all

16. Additional comments:

_____

_____

_____

Bibliography

Agosta, C. and Loring, M. (1988). Understanding and treating the adult retrospective victim of child sexual abuse. In Sgroi, S.M. (Ed.), *Vulnerable Populations: Evaluation and Treatment of Sexually Abused Children and Adult Survivors, Volume I.* Lexington, MA: Lexington Books, 115-135.

Alexander, P.C. and Follette, V.M. (1987). Personal constructs in the group treatment of incest. In Neimeyer, R.A. and Neimeyer, G.J. (Eds.), *Personal Construct Therapy Casebook.* New York: Springer, 211-229.

Alexander, P.C., Neimeyer, R.A., and Follette, V.M. (1991). Group therapy for women sexually abused as children: A controlled study and investigation of individual differences. *Journal of Interpersonal Violence, 6*(2), 218-231.

Allers, C.T. and Benjack, K.J. (1991). Connections between childhood abuse and HIV infection. *Journal of Counseling and Development, 70*(2), 309-313.

Alpert, J.L. (1990). Introduction to special section on clinical intervention in child sexual abuse. *Professional Psychology: Research and Practice, 21*(5), 323-324.

Alpert, J.L. (1995). *Sexual Abuse Recalled: Treating Trauma in the Era of the Recovered Memory Debate.* Northvale, NJ: Jason Aronson, Inc.

Alpert, J.L., Brown, L.S., Ceci, S.J., Courtois, C.A., Loftus, E.F., and Ornstein, P.A. (1996). *Final Report of the Working Group on Investigation of Memories of Childhood Abuse.* Washington, DC: American Psychological Association.

Alpert, J.L. and Paulson, A. (1990). Graduate-level education and training in child sexual abuse. *Professional Psychology: Research and Practice, 21*(5), 366-371.

Bacon, B. and Lein, L. (1996). Living with a sexual abuse survivor: Male partners perspectives. *Journal of Child Sexual Abuse, 5*(2), 1-15.

Bandura, A. (1977). Self-efficacy: Toward a unifying theory of behavioral change. *Psychological Review, 84*(2), 191-215.

Barbee, E.L. (1991). Ethnicity and woman abuse in the United States. In Sampselle, C.M. (Ed.), *Violence Against Women.* New York: Hemisphere Publishing Corporation, 153-166.

Bard, M. and Sangrey, D. (1986). *The Crime Victim's Book.* New York: Brunner/ Mazel.

Bass, E. and Davis, L. (1988). *The Courage to Heal.* New York: Harper & Row.

Becerra, R.M. and Iglehart, A.P. (1995). Intrafamilial child sexual abuse in the Hispanic community: A prevention approach. In Swift, C.F. (Ed.), *Sexual Assault and Abuse: Sociocultural Context of Prevention.* Binghamton, NY: The Haworth Press, 135-146.

Beitchman, J.H., Zucker, K.J., Hood, J.E., daCosta, G.A., Akman, D., and Cassavia, E. (1992). A review of the long-term effects of child sexual abuse. *Child Abuse and Neglect, 16*(1), 101-118.

Bergart, A.M. (1986). Isolation to intimacy: Incest survivors in group therapy. *Social Casework, 67*(5), 266-275.

Beutler, L.E. and Hill, C.E. (1992). Process and outcome research in the treatment of adult victims of childhood sexual abuse: Methodological issues. *Journal of Clinical and Consulting Psychology, 60*(2), 204-212.

Blake-White, J. and Kline, C.M. (1985). Treating the dissociative process in adult victims of childhood incest. *Social Casework, 66*(7), 394-402.

Blume, S.B. (1985). Group psychotherapy in the treatment of alcoholism. In Zimber, S., Wallace, J., and Blume, S. (Eds.), *Practical Approaches to Alcoholism Psychotherapy.* New York: Plenum Press, 73-85.

Bower, G.H. (1981). Mood and memory. *American Psychologist, 36*(2), 129-148.

Brandt, L.M. (1989). A short-term group therapy model for treatment of adult female survivors of childhood incest. *Group, 13*(2), 74-82.

Briere, J. (1989). *Therapy for Adults Molested as Children: Beyond Survival.* New York: Springer.

Briere, J. (1992). *Child Abuse Trauma: Theory and Treatment of the Lasting Effects.* Newbury Park, CA: Sage Publications.

Briere, J. (1998). Treating male survivors of sexual abuse. Workshop presented at APSAC conference, Child Sexual Abuse: A Multidisciplinary Training Conference for Law Enforcement, Child Protection, and Mental Health Professionals, Somerset, New Jersey, March.

Briere, J., Elliot, D., Harris, K., and Cotman, A. (1995). Trauma symptom inventory: Psychometrics and association with childhood and adult victims in clinical samples. *Journal of Interpersonal Violence, 10*(4), 387-401.

Briere, J. and Elliot, D. (1998). Clinical utility of the impact of events scale: Psychometrics in the general population. *Assessment, 5*(2), 171-180.

Briere, J. and Runtz, M. (1988). Post sexual abuse trauma. In Wyatt, G.E. and Powell, G.J. (Eds.), *Lasting Effects of Child Sexual Abuse.* Newbury Park, CA: Sage Publications, 85-100.

Browne, A. and Finkelhor, D. (1986). Impact of child sexual abuse: A review of the research. *Psychological Bulletin, 99*(1), 66-77.

Bruckner D.F. and Johnson, P.E. (1987). Treatment for adult male victims of childhood sexual abuse. *Social Casework, 68*(2), 81-87.

Cahill, C., Lewelyn, S.P., and Pearson, C. (1991). Long-term effects of childhood sexual abuse which occurred in childhood: A review. *British Journal of Clinical Psychology, 30*(2), 117-130.

Cahill, L., Prins, B., Weber, M., and McGaugh, J.L. (1994). B-adrenergic activation and memory for emotional events. *Nature, 371*(6499), 702-704.

Cameron, C. (1994). Women survivors confronting their abusers: Issues, decisions, and outcomes. *Journal of Child Sexual Abuse, 3*(1), 7-35.

Cantor, D.W. (1982). Children of divorce: Situation/transition group in the school. In Schaefer, C.E., Johnson, L., and Wherry, J.N. (Eds.), *Group Therapies for Children and Youth.* San Francisco: Jossey-Bass Publishers, 183-184.

Carmen, E.H., Reiker, P.P., and Mills, T. (1984). Victims of violence and psychiatric illness. *American Journal of Psychiatry, 141*(3), 378-379.

Ceci, S.J. and Bruck, M. (1995). *Jeopardy in the Courtroom: A Scientific Analysis of Children's Testimony.* Washington, DC: American Psychological Press.

Chauncey, S. (1994). Emotional concerns and treatment of male partners of sexual abuse survivors. *Social Work, 39*(6), 669-676.

Chew, J. (1998). *Women Survivors of Childhood Sexual Abuse: Healing Through Group Work.* Binghamton, NY: The Haworth Press.

Christianson, S.A. (1992). Emotional stress and eyewitness memory. *Psychological Bulletin, 112*(2), 284-309.

Coker, L.S. (1990). A therapeutic recovery model for the female adult incest survivor. *Issues in Mental Health Nursing, 11*(2), 109-123.

Cole, C.H. and Barney, E.E. (1987). Safeguards and the therapeutic window: A group treatment strategy for adult incest survivors. *American Journal of Orthopsychiatry, 57*(4), 601-609.

Cole, P.M. and Putnam, F.W. (1992). Effect of incest on self and social functioning: A developmental psychopathology perspective. *Journal of Consulting and Clinical Psychology, 60*(2), 174-184.

Courtois, C.A. (1979). The incest experience and its aftermath. *Victimology: An International Journal, 4,* 337-347.

Courtois, C.A. (1988). *Healing the Incest Wound.* New York: W.W. Norton and Company.

Courtois, C.A. (1991). Theory, sequencing, and strategy in treating adult survivors. In Briere, J.N. (Ed.), *Treating Victims of Child Sexual Abuse.* San Francisco: Jossey-Bass Publishers, 47-60.

Courtois, C.A. (1993). *Adult Survivors of Child Sexual Abuse.* Milwaukee, WI: Families International, Inc.

Courtois, C.A. and Sprei, J.E. (1988). Retrospective incest therapy for women. In Walker, L.E. (Ed.), *Handbook on Sexual Abuse of Children.* New York: Springer, 270-308.

Courtois, C.A. and Watts, D. (1982). Counseling adult women who experienced incest in childhood or adolescence. *Personnel and Guidance Journal, 60,* 275-279.

Dalenberg, C., Coe, M., Reto, M., Aransky, K., and Duvenage, C. (1995). The prediction of amnesiac barrier strength as an individual difference variable in state-dependent learning paradigms. Paper presented at a conference, Responding to Child Maltreatment, San Diego, California.

Deblinger, E., McLeer, S.V., and Henry, D. (1990). Cognitive-behavioral treatment for sexually abused children suffering post-traumatic stress: Preliminary findings. *Journal of the American Academy of Child Adolescent Psychiatry, 29*(5), 747-752.

Dinkmeyer, D.C. (1968). Group counseling. In Dinkmeyer, D.C. (Ed.), *Guidance and Counseling in the Elementary School: Readings in Therapy and Practice.* New York: Holt, Reinhart and Winston, Inc, 271-278.

Donaldson, M. and Cordes-Green, S. (1994). *Group Treatment of Adult Incest Survivors.* Thousand Oaks, CA: Sage Publications.

Doris, J. (Ed.) (1991). *The Suggestibility of Children's Recollections: Implications for Eyewitness Testimony.* Washington, DC: American Psychological Association.

Douglas, A.R. and Matson, I.C. (1989). An account of a time-limited therapeutic group in an NHS sets for women with a history of incest. *Group, 13*(2), 83-94.

Drews, J.R. and Bradley, J.T. (1989). Group therapy for adults molested as children: An educational and therapeutic approach. *Social Work with Groups, 12*(3), 57-75.

Elliott, D.M. and Briere, J. (1992). The sexually abused boy: Problems in manhood. *Medical Aspects of Human Sexuality, 26*(2), 68-71.

Epstein, S. (1985). The implications of cognitive-experiential self-theory for research in social psychology and personality. *Journal for the Theory of Social Behavior, 15,* 283-310.

Erickson, E.H. (1980). *Identity and the Life Cycle.* New York: W.W. Norton and Company.

False Memory Syndrome Foundation (FMSF) (1992). Information needed in assessing allegation by adults of sex abuse in childhood. *False Memory Syndrome Foundation Newsletter,* November 5, 5.

Fine, C. (1990). The cognitive sequelae of incest. In Kluft, R.P. (Ed.), *Incest-Related Syndromes of Adult Psychopathology.* Washington, DC: American Psychiatric Press, 161-182.

Finkelhor, D. (1979). *Sexually Victimized Children.* New York: Free Press.

Finkelhor, D. (1990). Early and long term effects of childhood sexual abuse: An update. *Professional Psychology: Research and Practice, 21*(5), 325-330.

Finkelhor, D. and Berliner, L. (1995). Research on treatment of sexually abused children: A review and recommendations. *Journal of the American Academy of Child and Adolescent Psychiatry, 34*(11), 1408-1423.

Finkelhor, D. and Browne, A. (1985). The traumatic impact of child sexual abuse: A conceptualization. *American Journal of Orthopsychiatry, 55*(4), 530-541.

Finkelhor, D., Hotaling, G., Lewis, I.A., and Smith, C. (1989). Sexual abuse and its relationship to later sexual satisfaction, marital status, religion, and attitudes. *Journal of Interpersonal Violence, 4*(4), 279-399.

Firth, M.T. (1997). Male partners of female victims of child sexual abuse: Treatment issues and approaches. *Sexual and Marital Therapy, 12*(2), 159-172.

Fish-Murray, C.C., Koby, E.V., and van der Kolk, B.A. (1987). Evolving ideas: The effect of abuse on children's thought. In van der Kolk, B.A. (Ed.), *Psychological Trauma.* Washington, DC: American Psychiatric Press, 89-110.

Flannery, R.B. (1987). From victim to survivor: A stress management approach in the treatment of learned helplessness. In van der Kolk, B.A. (Ed.), *Psychological Trauma.* Washington, DC: American Psychiatric Press, 217-232.

Foa, E.B., Steketee, G., and Rothbaum, B.O. (1989). Behavioral/cognitive conceptualizations of post-traumatic stress disorder. *Behavior Therapy, 20*(2), 155-176.

Follette, V.M., Alexander, P.C., and Follette, W.C. (1991). Individual predictors of outcome in group treatment for incest survivors. *Journal of Consulting and Clinical Psychology, 59*(1), 150-155.

Freud, S. (1905). Three essays on the theory of sexuality. In Strachey, J. (Ed.), *The Standard Edition of the Complete Works of Freud, Volume Seven.* London: Hogarth Press, 125-143.

Freyd, J. (1996). *Betrayal Trauma Theory: The Logic of Forgetting Abuse.* Cambridge, MA: Harvard University Press.

Friedrich, W.N. (1988). Behavior problems in sexually abused children. In Wyatt, G.E. and Powell, G.J. (Eds.), *Lasting Effects of Child Sexual Abuse.* Newbury Park, CA: Sage Publications, 171-192.

Friedrich, W.N. (1995). *Psychotherapy with Sexually Abused Boys: An Integrated Approach.* Thousand Oaks, CA: Sage Publications.

Galinsky, M. and Schopler, J.H. (1977). Warning: Groups may be dangerous. *Social Work, 22*(2), 89-94.

Gartner, R.B. (1997). An analytic group for sexually abused men. *International Journal of Group Psychotherapy, 47*(3), 373-383.

Gazan, M. (1986). An evaluation of a treatment package designed for women with a history of sexual victimization in childhood and sexual dysfunction in adulthood. *Canadian Journal of Community Mental Health, 5*(2), 85-101.

Gelinas, D.J. (1983). The persisting negative effects of incest. *Psychiatry, 46*(4), 312-332.

Gold-Steinberg, S. and Buttenheim, M.C. (1993). "Telling one's story" in an incest survivors group. *International Journal of Group Psychotherapy, 43*(2), 173-189.

Gomes-Schwartz, B., Horowitz, J., and Sauzier, M. (1985). Severity of emotional disturbance among sexually abused preschool, school age, and adolescent children. *Hospital Community Psychiatry, 36*(5) 503-508.

Goodman,·B. and Nowack-Scibelli, D.(1985). Group treatment for women incestuously abused as children. *International Journal of Group Psychotherapy, 35*(4), 531-544.

Goodwin, J. (1982). *Sexual Abuse: Incest Victims and Their Families.* Littleton, MA: PGS Publishing.

Goodwin, J.M. (1990). Applying to adult incest victims what we have learned from victimized children. In Kluft, R.P. (Ed.), *Incest-Related Syndromes of Adult Psychopathology.* Washington, DC: American Psychiatric Press, 55-74.

Goodwin, J.M. and Talwar, N. (1989). Group psychotherapy for victims of incest. *Psychiatric Clinics of North America, 12*(2), 279-293.

Hall, R.P., Kassees, J.M., and Hoffman, C. (1986). Treatment for survivors of incest. *Journal for Specialists in Group Work, 11*(2), 85-92.

Hampton, R. (1987). Violence against black children: Current knowledge and future research needs. In Hampton, R. (Ed.), *Violence in the Black Family.* Lexington, MA: DC Heath, 3-20.

Hansen, P.A. (1991). *Survivors and Partners: Healing the Relationships of Sexual Abuse Survivors.* Longmont, CO: Heron Hill Publishing Company.

Harrison, J.B. (1998). Author and clinical psychologist. Personal communication.

Harrison, J.B. and Morris, L.A. (1995). Group therapy treatment for male survivors of sexual child abuse. In Andronico, M. (Ed.), *Men in Groups.* Washington, DC: American Psychological Press, 339-356.

Harvey, J.H. and Parks, M.M. (1981). *Psychotherapy Research and Behavior Change.* Washington, DC: American Psychological Association.

Hays, K.F. (1985). Electra in mourning: Grief work and the adult incest survivor. *Psychotherapy Patient, 2*(1), 45-58.

Herman, J.L. (1992). *Trauma and Recovery.* New York: Basic Books.

Herman, J. and Hirschman, L. (1981). *Father-Daughter Incest.* Cambridge, MA: Harvard University Press.

Herman, J. and Schatzow, E. (1984). Time-limited group therapy for women with a history of incest. *International Journal of Group Psychotherapy, 34*(4), 605-616.

Herman, J. and Schatzow, E. (1987). Recovery and verification of memories of childhood sexual trauma. *Psychoanalytic Psychology, 4*(1), 1-14.

Herman, J. and van der Kolk, B. (1987). Traumatic antecedents of borderline personality disorder. In van der Kolk, B.A. (Ed.), *Psychological Trauma*, 111-126. Washington, DC: American Psychiatric Press.

Hunter, M. (1990). *Abused Boys: The Neglected Victims of Sexual Abuse.* Lexington, MA: Lexington Books.

Hunter, M. (Ed.) (1995). *Adult Survivors of Sexual Abuse: Treatment Innovations.* Thousand Oaks, CA: Sage Publications.

Janoff-Bulman, R. and Frieze, I. (1983). A theoretical perspective for understanding reactions to victimization. *Journal of Social Issues, 39*(2), 1-18.

Jehu, D. (1988). *Beyond Sexual Abuse: Therapy with Women Who Were Victims in Childhood.* Chichester, England: Wiley.

Kempe, R.S. and Kempe, C.H. (1984). *The Common Secret: Sexual Abuse of Children and Adolescents.* New York: Freeman.

Kluft, R.P. (1990). *Incest-Related Syndromes of Adult Psychopathology.* Washington, DC: American Psychiatric Press.

Kohut, H. (1971). *The Analysis of Self.* New York: International Universities Press.

Koss, M.P., Tromp, S., and Tharan, M. (1995). Traumatic memories: Empirical foundations, forensic and clinical implications. *Clinical Psychology: Science and Practice, 2*(2), 111-132.

Kreidler, M.C. and England, D.B. (1990). Empowerment through group support: Adult women who are survivors of incest. *Journal of Family Violence, 5*(1), 35-42.

Ladwig, G.B. and Andersen, M.D. (1991). Substance abuse in women: Relationship between chemical dependency of women and past reports of physical and/or sexual abuse. In Sampselle, C.M. (Ed.), *Violence Against Women.* New York: Hemisphere Publishing Corporation, 167-180.

Laidlaw, T. and Malmo, C. (1990). *Healing Voices: Feminist Approaches to Therapy with Women.* San Francisco: Jossey-Bass Publishers.

LeBlanc, A.N. (1993). Harassment at school: The truth is out. *Seventeen,* May, 134-135.

Lew, M. (1990). *Victims No Longer: Men Recovering from Incest and Other Childhood Sexual Abuse.* New York: Harper & Row.

Lindsay, D.S. and Briere, J. (1997). The controversy regarding recovered memories of childhood sexual abuse. *Journal of Interpersonal Violence, 12*(5), 631-647.

Lisak, D. (1995). Integrating a critique of gender in the treatment of male survivors of childhood sexual abuse. *Psychotherapy, 32*(2), 258-269.

Loftus, E.F. (1988). *Memory: Surprising New Insights into How We Remember and Why We Forget.* New York: Ardsley House.

Loftus, E.F. (1993). The reality of repressed memories. *American Psychologist, 48*(5), 518-537.

Maddock, J.W. and Larson, N.R. (1995). *Incestuous Families.* New York: W.W. Norton and Company.

Maher, C.A. (1977). Professional school psychology: A perspective. *New Jersey Psychologist, 28,* 9-12.

Maher, C.A. and Bennett, R.E. (1984). *Planning and Evaluating Special Education Services.* Englewood Cliffs, NJ: Prentice-Hall.

Mahler, M., Pine, F., and Bergman, A. (1975). *The Psychological Birth of the Human Infant.* New York: Basic Books.

Mahoney, M.J. (1981). Psychotherapy and human change process. In Harvey, J.H. and Parks, M.M. (Eds.), *Psychotherapy Research and Behavior Change.* Washington, DC: American Psychological Association, 73-122.

Maltz, W. (1991). *The Sexual Healing Journey: A Guide for Survivors of Sexual Abuse.* New York: HarperCollins Publishers.

Mandell, J.G., Damon, L., Castaldo, P.C., Tauber, E.S., Monise, L., and Larsen, N.F. (1989). *Group Treatment for Sexually Abused Children.* New York: The Guilford Press.

Mann, D. (1992). Male Victimization Workshop presented at Institute for Advanced Clinical Training, Baltimore, MD.

Mann, J. (1973). *Time-Limited Psychotherapy.* Cambridge, MA: Harvard University Press.

Mann, T. (1991). Episodic memory in people with mental retardation. *Dissertation Abstracts, 52*(3), 1749.

McBride, M.C. and Markos, P.A. (1994). Sources of difficulty in counseling sexual abuse victims and survivors. *Canadian Journal of Counseling, 28*(1), 83-99.

McCann, I.L., Pearlman, L.A., Sakheim, D.K., and Abrahamson, D.J. (1988). Assessment and treatment of the adult survivor of childhood sexual abuse within a schema framework. In Sgroi, S.M. (Ed.), *Vulnerable Populations: Evaluation and Treatment of Sexually Abused Children and Adult Survivors, Volume I.* Lexington, MA: Lexington Books, 77-101.

McCann, I.L. and Pearlman, L.A. (1990). *Psychological Trauma and the Adult Survivor: Theory, Therapy, and Transformation.* New York: Brunner/Mazel.

McCarthy, B. (1986). A cognitive-behavioral approach to understanding and treating sexual trauma. *Journal of Sex and Marital Therapy, 12*(4), 322-328.

Meichenbaum, D. (1985). Stress inoculation: A preventative approach. *Issues in Mental Health Nursing, 7*(14), 419-435.

Meiselman, K.C. (1990). *Resolving the Trauma of Incest.* San Francisco: Jossey-Bass Publishers.

Mendel, M.P. (1995). *The Male Survivor: The Impact of Sexual Abuse.* Thousand Oaks, CA: Sage Publications.

Mennen, F.E. (1994). The relationship of race/ethnicity to symptoms in childhood sexual abuse. *Child Abuse and Neglect, 19*(1), 115-124.

Mennen, F.E. and Meadow, D. (1992). Process to recovery: In support of long-term groups for sexual abuse survivors. *International Journal of Group Psychotherapy, 42*(4), 29-44.

Miller, A. (1981). *Prisoners of Childhood: The Drama of the Gifted Child and the Search for the True Self.* New York: Basic Books.

Pearlman, L.A. and Saakvitne, K.W. (1995). *Trauma and the Therapist: Countertransference and Vicarious Traumatization in Psychotherapy with Incest Survivors.* New York: W.W. Norton.

Pearson, Q.M. (1994). Treatment techniques for adult female survivors of childhood sexual abuse. *Journal of Counseling and Development, 73*(1), 32-37.

Pezdek, K. and Roe, C. (1994). Memory for childhood events: How suggestible is it? *Consciousness and Cognition, 3*(3-4), 374-387.

Piaget, J. (1967). *Six Psychological Studies.* New York: Vintage Books.

Pope, K.S. and Brown, L.S. (1996). *Recovered Memories of Abuse: Assessment, Therapy, Forensics.* Washington, DC: American Psychological Association, 23-65.

Pope, K.S. and Feldman-Summers, S. (1992). National survey of psychologists' sexual and physical abuse history and their evaluation of training and competence in these areas. *Professional Psychology: Research and Practice, 23*(5), 353-361.

Price, M. (1994). Incest: Transference and countertransference implications. *Journal of the American Academy of Psychoanalysis, 22*(2), 211-229.

Putnam, F. and Tricket, P. (1993). Impact of child sexual abuse on females: Toward a developmental, psychobiological integration. *Psychological Science, 4*(2),81-87.

Reed, B. (1985). Drug misuse and dependency in women: The meaning and implications of being considered a special population or minority group. *International Journal of the Addictions, 20*(1), 13-62.

Rieker, P. and Carmen, E. (1986). The victim to patient process: The disconfirmation and transformation of abuse. *American Journal of Orthopsychiatry, 56*(3), 360-370.

Roberts, L. and Lie, G.Y. (1989). A group therapy approach to the treatment of incest. *Social Work with Groups, 12*(3), 77-90.

Ross, C.A. (1989). *Multiple Personality Disorder.* New York: John Wiley and Sons.

Roth, S. and Newman, E. (1991). The process of coping with sexual trauma. *Journal of Traumatic Stress, 4*(2), 279-297.

Rush, F. (1977). The Freudian cover-up. *Chrysalis, 1*, 31-45.

Russell, D.E. (1986). *The Secret Trauma: Incest in the Lives of Girls and Women.* New York: Basic Books.

Russell, D.E., Schurman, R.A., and Trocki, K. (1988). The long-term effects of incestuous abuse: A comparison of Afro-American and white American victims. In Wyatt, G.E. and Powell, G.J. (Eds.), *Lasting Effects of Child Sexual Abuse.* Newbury Park, CA: Sage Publications, 119-134.

Sampselle, C.M. (Ed.) (1991). *Violence Against Women.* New York: Hemisphere Publishing Corporation.

Sanders-Philips, K., Moisan, P.A., Wadlington, S., Morgan, S., and English, K. (1995). Ethnic differences in psychological functioning among black and Latino sexually abused girls. *Child Abuse and Neglect, 9*(6), 691-706.

Sansonnet-Hayden, H., Haley, G., and Marriage, K. (1987). Sexual abuse and psychopathology in hospitalized adolescents. *Journal of American Academy of Child Psychiatry, 26*(5), 753-757.

Schatzow, E. and Herman, J. (1989). Breaking secrecy: Adult survivors disclose to their families. *Psychiatric Clinics of North America, 12*(2), 337-349.

Schetky, D.H. (1990). A review of the literature on the long-term effects of childhood sexual abuse. In Kluft, R.P. (Ed.), *Incest-Related Syndromes of Adult Psychopathology.* Washington, DC: American Psychiatric Press, 35-54.

Sedney, M.A. and Brooks, B. (1984). Factors associated with a history of childhood sexual experience in a nonclinical female population. *Journal of the American Academy of Child Psychiatry, 23*(2), 215-218.

Sgroi, S.M. (Ed.) (1988) *Vulnerable Populations: Evaluation and Treatment of Sexually Abused Children and Adult Survivors, Volume I.* Lexington, MA: Lexington Books.

Sgroi, S.M. and Bunk, B.S. (1988). A clinical approach to adult survivors of child sexual abuse. In Sgroi, S.M. (Ed.), *Vulnerable Populations: Evaluation and Treatment of Sexually Abused Children and Adult Survivors, Volume I.* Lexington, MA: Lexington Books, 137-186.

Singer, K.I. (1989). Group work with men who experienced incest in childhood. *American Journal of Orthopsychiatry, 59*(3), 468-472.

Slater, B.R. and Gallagher, M.M. (1989). Outside the realm of psychotherapy: Consultation for interventions with sexualized children. *School Psychology Review, 18*(3), 400-411.

Stein, J.A., Golding, J.M., Siegel, J.M., Burnam, M.A., and Sorenson, S.B. (1988). Long-term psychological sequelae of child sexual abuse: The Los Angeles Epidemiologic Catchment Area Study. In Wyatt, G.E. and Powell, G.J. (Eds.), *Lasting Effects of Child Sexual Abuse.* Newbury Park, CA: Sage Publications, 135-154.

Stone, M.H. (1989). Individual psychotherapy with victims of incest. *Psychiatric Clinics of North America, 12*(2), 237-255.

Swift, C.F. (1995). *Sexual Assault and Abuse: Sociocultural Context of Prevention.* Binghamton, NY: The Haworth Press.

Swink, K.K. and Leveille, A.E. (1986). From victim to survivor: A new look at the issues and recovery process for adult incest survivors. *Women and Therapy, 5*(2-3), 119-141.

Tharinger, D. (1990). Impact of child sexual abuse on developing sexuality. *Professional Psychology: Research and Practice, 21*(5), 331-337.

Thomas, M.C., Nelson, C.S., and Sumners, C.M. (1994). From victims to victors: Group process as the path to recovery for males molested as children. *Journal for Specialists in Group Work, 19*(2), 102-111.

Trepper, T.S. and Barrett, M. (1989). *Systemic Treatment of Incest: A Therapeutic Handbook.* New York: Brunner/Mazel.

Urquiza, A. and Crowley, C. (1986). Sex differences in the survivors of childhood sexual abuse. Paper presented at the Fourth National Conference on the Victimization of Children, New Orleans, May.

van der Kolk, B.A. (Ed.) (1987a). *Psychological Trauma.* Washington, DC: American Psychiatric Press.

van der Kolk, B.A. (1987b). The role of the group in the origin and resolution of the trauma response. In van der Kolk, B.A. (Ed.), *Psychological Trauma.* Washington, DC: American Psychiatric Press, 153-171.

van der Kolk, B.A. and Saporta, J. (1991). The biological response to psychic trauma: Mechanics and treatment of intrusion and numbing. *Anxiety Research, 4*(3), 199-212.

Wadsworth, R., Spampneto, A.M., and Halbrook, B.M. (1995). The role of sexual trauma in the treatment of chemically dependent women: Addressing the relapse issue. *Journal of Counseling and Development, 73*(4), 401-406.

Waites, E.A. (1993). *Trauma and Survival: Post-traumatic and Dissociative Disorders in Women.* New York: W.W. Norton and Company.

Webb, L.P. and Leehan, J. (1996). *Group Treatment for Adult Survivors of Abuse: A Manual for Practitioners.* Thousand Oaks, CA: Sage Publications.

Westerlund, E. (1992). *Women's Sexuality After Childhood Incest.* New York: W.W. Norton and Company.

Wilson, K. and James, A. (1992). Child sexual abuse and couple therapy. *Sexual and Marital Therapy, 7*(2), 197-212.

Wilson, M. (1994). *Crossing the Boundary: Black Women Survive Incest.* Seattle, WA: Seal Press.

Wyatt, G. (1985). *Resolving the Trauma of Incest.* San Francisco: Jossey-Bass Publishers.

Wyatt, G.E. (1986). The relationship between the cumulative impact of a range of child sexual abuse experiences and women's psychological well-being. *Victimology: An International Journal, 1*(4).

Wyatt, G.E. (1990). The aftermath of child sexual abuse of African American and white American women: The victim's experience. *Journal of Family Violence, 5*(1), 61-81.

Wyatt, G.E. and Powell, G.J. (Eds.) (1988). *Lasting Effects of Child Sexual Abuse.* Newbury Park, CA: Sage Publications.

Wyatt, G.E., Notgrass, C.M., and Gordon, G. (1995). The effects of African American women's sexual revictimization: Strategies for prevention. In Swift, C.F. (Ed.), *Sexual Assault and Abuse: Sociocultural Context of Prevention.* Binghamton, NY: The Haworth Press, 111-134.

Wylie, M.S. (1993). The shadow of a doubt. *The Family Therapy Networker, 17*(5), 18-29.

Yalom, I. (1975). *The Theory and Practice of Group Psychotherapy* (Second Edition). New York: Basic Books.

Yamamoto-Nading, D. and Stringer, G.M. (1991). *A Healing Celebration.* Renton, WA: King County Sexual Assault Resource Center.

Yates, J.L. and Nasby, W. (1993). Dissociation, affect and network models of memory: An integrative proposal. *Journal of Traumatic Stress, 6*(3), 305-326.

Yehuda, R., Kahana, B., Binder-Brnes, K., Southwick, S., Mason, J.W., and Giller, E.L. (1995). Low urinary cortisol excretion in Holocaust survivors with post-traumatic stress disorder. *American Journal of Psychiatry, 152*(7), 982-986.

Zaragoza, M.S. (1991). Preschool children's susceptibility to memory impairment. In Doris, J. (Ed.), *The Suggestibility of Children's Recollections: Implications for Eyewitness Testimony.* Washington, DC: American Psychological Association, 27-39.

Index

Page numbers followed by the letter "t" indicate tables.

Order Your Own Copy of
This Important Book for Your Personal Library!

BREAKING THE SILENCE
Group Therapy for Childhood Sexual Abuse, A Practitioner's Manual

_____ in hardbound at $29.95 (ISBN: 0-7890-0200-0)

COST OF BOOKS_____

OUTSIDE USA/CANADA/
MEXICO: ADD 20%_____

POSTAGE & HANDLING_____
(US: $3.00 for first book & $1.25
for each additional book)
Outside US: $4.75 for first book
& $1.75 for each additional book)

SUBTOTAL_____

IN CANADA: ADD 7% GST_____

STATE TAX_____
(NY, OH & MN residents, please
add appropriate local sales tax)

FINAL TOTAL_____
(If paying in Canadian funds,
convert using the current
exchange rate. UNESCO
coupons welcome.)

☐ **BILL ME LATER:** ($5 service charge will be added)
(Bill-me option is good on US/Canada/Mexico orders only;
not good to jobbers, wholesalers, or subscription agencies.)

☐ Check here if billing address is different from
shipping address and attach purchase order and
billing address information.

Signature_____

☐ **PAYMENT ENCLOSED: $**_____

☐ **PLEASE CHARGE TO MY CREDIT CARD.**

☐ Visa   ☐ MasterCard   ☐ AmEx   ☐ Discover
☐ Diner's Club

Account #_____

Exp. Date_____

Signature_____

Prices in US dollars and subject to change without notice.

NAME _____

INSTITUTION _____

ADDRESS _____

CITY _____

STATE/ZIP _____

COUNTRY _____ COUNTY (NY residents only) _____

TEL _____ FAX _____

E-MAIL_____
May we use your e-mail address for confirmations and other types of information? ☐ Yes   ☐ No

Order From Your Local Bookstore or Directly From
The Haworth Press, Inc.
10 Alice Street, Binghamton, New York 13904-1580 • USA
TELEPHONE: 1-800-HAWORTH (1-800-429-6784) / Outside US/Canada: (607) 722-5857
FAX: 1-800-895-0582 / Outside US/Canada: (607) 772-6362
E-mail: getinfo@haworthpressinc.com
PLEASE PHOTOCOPY THIS FORM FOR YOUR PERSONAL USE.

BOF96

SUNY BROCKPORT

3 2815 00813 9068

RC 569 .5 .A28 M37 1999

Margolin, Judith A.

Breaking the silence

DATE DUE

MAR 2 1 2001		
AUG 1 5 2001		
AUG 1 6 2001		
MAY 0 7 2003		
APR 2 6 2003		
FEB 1 7 2006		
MAR 2 7 2012		
NOV 03 2012		
NOV 2 6 2012		

GAYLORD   PRINTED IN U.S.A